Twayne's United States Authors Series

Sylvia E. Bowman, *Editor*

INDIANA UNIVERSITY

Richard Watson Gilder

RICHARD WATSON GILDER

By HERBERT F. SMITH

The University of Wisconsin

 166

Twayne Publishers, Inc.   ::   New York

To
Virginia

To
Virginia

Preface

THE SECOND American renaissance, comparable at all points to the first, which F. O. Mattheissen described, can be dated at approximately 1880–1885. This second renaissance had as its operating esthetic the rise of realism; its great practitioners were William Dean Howells, Mark Twain, and Henry James; its literary function was to prove the maturity of American letters. To a considerable extent, this renaissance took place on the pages of the magazine directed by Richard Watson Gilder, *The Century*. It was a time of great editors: B. O. Flower of *The Arena*, Henry Mills Alden of *Harper's*, Horace Scudder and Thomas Bailey Aldrich of *The Atlantic*. Somehow, Gilder managed to be the most successful of these, to make his magazine the vehicle for the most significant statements of the renaissance, to develop new young writers from the South and West as a kind of backdrop for the great works on the center stage, and to create the esthetic for the masterpieces written around 1885.

The purpose of this study is to observe and analyze Gilder as an editor-critic of literature in the making. To this end, Chapter One examines the conditions of American literature during Gilder's lifetime, with special attention to the literary marketplace and the position of the magazine. The second chapter considers Gilder as a poet and an editor of poetry, concentrating upon his relationship with the one great poet of his lifetime, Walt Whitman. The third chapter deals with his part in another renaissance, this one of the post-Civil War southern writers, especially George Washington Cable and Joel Chandler Harris, whose writing he helped to shape. Chapter Four illustrates the way in which Gilder championed American writing at the expense of English contributors, and Chapters Five, Six, and Seven analyze his treatment of western writers, William Dean Howells and Mark Twain in particular. The final chapter is a consideration of his esthetic theory in general and a summary and analysis of his influence and significance in American literature.

I wish to thank the Wisconsin Research Council for its assistance in the pursuance of this subject; professors Rudolf and Clara Kirk and Henry Pochmann for aid and comfort at various stages of the composition; and Professor Sylvia Bowman for her editorial assistance.

HERBERT F. SMITH

University of Wisconsin

Contents

Contents

Chronology

1844   February 8, Richard Watson Gilder born in Bordentown, New Jersey.

1868   Edited *Poems by Ellen Clementine Howarth.*

1869   Joined editorial staff of *Hours at Home;* succeeded James M. Sherwood as editor-in-chief.

1870   November, first issue of *Scribner's Monthly Magazine;* Gilder managing editor under Josiah G. Holland.

1874   June 3, married Helena DeKay.

1875   Published *The New Day.*

1878   Published *The Poet and His Master.*

1879–   First trip to Europe. Met Frederic Mistral, and became a
1880   member of the *Societé des Félibriges;* met Robert Browning, Swinburne, and other literati in London.

1881   October, death of Josiah Holland; Gilder became editor-in-chief of *The Century Magazine,* first issue, November.

1883   Founding of the International Copyright League.

1885   Published *Lyrics.* High point of *The Century* with publication of "Battles and Leaders of the Civil War," extensive contributions by James, Twain, Howells, others.

1891   Published *Two Worlds;* passage of international copyright treaty.

1891–   Extensive social and reform work: for civil service reform,
1895   Tenement House Commission, Anti-Spoils League, etc.

1894   Published *Five Books of Song.*

1895   Second voyage to Europe and the Near East.

1900   Third trip to Europe.

1906   Published *A Book of Music.*

1908   Published *Poems,* first volume in Houghton Mifflin's series of "Household Poets" by a living poet.

1909   Died, November 18, New York City.

1916   Rosamond Gilder edited *Letters of Richard Watson Gilder.*

CHAPTER *1*

The Man, The Magazine

FOR thirty-nine of the most eventful years in American literature, 1870–1909, Richard Watson Gilder controlled or helped
to control the fortunes of one of the most influential magazines in
America. As assistant editor of *Scribner's Monthly Magazine* and
as editor-in-chief of its successor, *The Century Monthly Magazine*,
he rose to a position of editorial importance second to no man of
the period. Indeed, were it not for the pun and the inexplicable
neglect of Gilder by modern literary historians, the decade of his
greatest power, roughly 1880–1890, might well be called the
"Gilder Age." For those ten years the family magazine was the most
powerful literary force in America, the best of all these magazines
was *The Century*, and the ruler of *The Century* was Gilder. But,
because he came to be accepted as a symbol of the "genteel tradition," Gilder has been overlooked in too many studies, cultu-
ral, historical, and literary, of his age.

Doubtless one of the reasons Gilder's influence upon American
literature has never been adequately studied is simply that he is
primarily an editor, and not a poet, critic, or novelist. Poets, critics, and novelists leave a corpus of work by which they may be
judged and from which their influence may be inferred. An editor,
from one point of view at least, may be no more obtrusively present in the structure of the literature of his period than the midwife
who presided at his birth may be for the biography of a great
man. Yet, from another and more profound point of view, an editor or a number of editors—and Gilder is only among the most
prominent in an age of great editors—does more to shape the literature of a period than any single writer could possibly do. This
study is based upon two assumptions which seem to be self-evi-
dent: first, that an editor is by nature a critic, that he performs all
the functions of a critic and is, in fact, more powerful than a critic
in his effect upon literature because his critical judgments are not

given *ex post facto*, but of the literature, as it were, in the bud. Second, that as we judge a critic by his writings, by the product of opinions he produces, so must we judge an editor by his productions: the magazine he creates, the literary choices that go into its creation. This study is an application of those two assumptions to Gilder. I shall examine his relationships with significant writers of his day—his treatment of their writings, his choices among them for his magazine, his opinions and commentary upon them—as if they were formal critical expressions. For, if these relationships lack something in literary merit for themselves, they are nevertheless important as formative policies in the very creation of American literature. Through such an examination, we may see how Gilder was a force in American literary development, we may dispel the myth of his symbolic personification of the "genteel tradition," and we may finally come to evaluate him personally as a poet, critic-editor, and man of letters.

I *Of Men* . . .

Gilder was born in Bordentown, New Jersey, on February 8, 1844. His father, the Reverend William Henry Gilder, was a Methodist minister and proprietor and headmaster of a girls' school, first in Bordentown and later in Flushing, Long Island, New York. During the first fourteen years of his life Richard acquired nearly all his education in his father's "Flushing Female Academy," where he was the only male student. The psychological implications of that period upon his later career may be left to the Freudians; the evidence suggests he had an unusually happy boyhood, including largely male interests and precocious capabilities. When he was only twelve years old, he began to frequent the office of the Flushing *Long Island Times.* He learned the routines of publishing, even set type for several issues of the paper. Later, while still in his early teens, he produced two amateur newspapers of his own, the *St. Thomas Register* and *The Leaflet,* both of which show the rudiments of good editorial judgment.

Adult responsibility was forced upon Gilder while he was still young. At eighteen he enlisted as a private in the Philadelphia Artillery, a militia organization, but saw brief and hardly warlike service during the summer of 1863. The closest he came to action was helping in the defense of Harrisburg while General Lee was at Gettysburg. The impact of the Civil War came to him, not through his militia activities, which were more in the nature of a boyish lark, but with his father's death from smallpox, contracted in the line of duty as a chaplain in the Federal army. The death of his father forced Gilder to return to his family to take over the duties of its head. For a short time he worked as paymaster on the Camden and Amboy Railroad, spending more time reading poetry than doing his work. At this time he became acquainted with Ellen Clementine Howarth, a Newark poetess, and in 1867 he edited a volume of her poems, for which he wrote an eight-page introduction.

Shortly after the volume appeared, he became a reporter on the *Newark Advertiser.* His stay there was brief, for early in 1869 he joined Robert Newton Crane, an uncle of Stephen Crane, in the founding of the Newark *Morning Register.* The *Register* paid no salary in its first years; so, to make ends meet, Gilder got a second job as an editor for *Hours at Home,* a monthly publication of Charles Scribner and Company. The *Morning Register* survived until 1878, but Gilder divorced himself from it shortly after joining *Hours at Home.* Within a few months he became sole editor of *Hours at Home,* and he remained in that position through the last year of the magazine's life, from November, 1869, to October, 1870.

Gilder, who was only twenty-five years old when he joined the staff of *Hours at Home,* was not quite twenty-six when he became editor-in-chief. The magazine was, to say the least, modest in its aspirations. Its circulation was limited; its purpose was primarily to stimulate the sale of books by authors contracted to Charles Scribner and Company and to provide an outlet for shorter works by those authors. Its ninety-six pages of nine-point type included articles like Horace Bushnell's "The Moral Uses of Dark Things," pirated novels by English authors like Charlotte Yonge's *The Chaplet of Pearls,* and unsigned poems with titles like "The Duration of Bliss," "The Rivulet," and "Evening at Cape Ann."

The editor who preceded Gilder, James Murray Sherwood, favored theological writings more than did Gilder; but Sherwood's choice of foreign writings for the magazine, notably Tolstoi's *Sevastopol Sketches,* shows that he could recognize literary merit, even if, under the copyright laws of the day, he did not have to pay for it. Gilder made no great improvements in the magazine upon becoming its editor; no editor could. The mediocrity of the magazine was a product of the philosophy behind it. Modeled upon *Harper's Magazine* (which at this early date shared many of its faults), the magazine was held completely subordinate to its parent publishing firm. What it needed was an expanded investment for more original material, a more interesting and readable format, judicious illustrations (there were none in *Hours at Home* except for an occasional frontispiece), and an existence less dependent upon Charles Scribner and Company.

But Charles Scribner thought that a prominent editor could build up the magazine, and to that end in 1868 asked the popular writer, Josiah Gilbert Holland, to take over. By this action Scribner was not reflecting upon Gilder's editorial capacity except in terms of his youth and his lack of a literary reputation. Scribner hoped to interest the thousands of readers of Holland's books in the magazine, to increase the circulation without radically changing the format or the expense. Holland only promised to consider the offer and left for a tour of Europe. It was during that tour that *Scribner's Monthly Magazine* was born.

Coincidence brought Holland and Roswell C. Smith together in Geneva in 1869. Smith, who had made a fortune in western real estate, had "retired" from business at the age of thirty-nine to make an extended tour of Europe. For Holland, success had come much later in life; but, at the time of his European vacation in 1868–1869, he was at a peak of popularity as a writer of moral essays for young people. His *Timothy Titcomb's Letters to Young People, Single and Married* sold over fifty thousand copies in ten years, and he acquired a following that insured the success of any book he wrote. Holland, undecided whether to accept Scribner's offer to edit *Hours at Home*, asked Smith's advice, and the idea for *Scribner's Monthly* resulted. The new magazine was to be more ambitiously designed and executed than *Hours at Home*, edited by Holland and managed by Smith, with Scribner supplying only the imprint and title.

Scribner agreed to the plan when it was presented to him, and a new organization, Scribner and Company, was formed. Stock was divided thirty percent each to Holland and Smith and forty percent to Scribner, and the new company was to be totally separate from Charles Scribner and Company. The transaction took place late in 1869, but the founders decided not to begin the new venture until the termination in November, 1870, of the next complete volume of *Hours at Home*. Gilder was to continue as editor of the old magazine until its termination, when he would become assistant editor of the new magazine under Holland.

The agreement left Gilder in what might seem to be an unenviable position. Responsible for the last twelve issues of the old magazine, he began as early as January, 1870, to help Holland plan for the first issues of *Scribner's Monthly*. His work for the new magazine was not, however, extensive; Holland solicited contributions from the many literary men and women he knew—a project in which Gilder took no part except to read some of the manuscripts. Nor did Holland interfere with the production of *Hours at Home* except to ask Gilder not to improve the physical appearance of the old magazine during its final year so that the new magazine might profit by the contrast.[1] In general the transition went smoothly, and the first issue of *Scribner's Monthly* presented a striking new appearance when compared to its humble predecessor. It had a new cover design, a more readable format, well-chosen and well-executed illustrations, and, most important of all, writings by authors known to the subscribers.

The new magazine reflected the character of its new editor-in-chief. Holland had no fear of controversy or criticism. When someone suggested that the magazine eschew such controversial subjects as religion and politics, he replied that he did not "intend to cut the magazine off from the resources of popularity and influence" which the treatment of controversial subjects could bring to the magazine, but would strive not to be "partisan or dogmatic" about such issues. "Harper's monopolizes the market for harmless and inoffensive literary pap," he observed. His magazine would instead "boldly lead in the denunciation of social and political abuses from the Christian standpoint."[2] *Scribner's Monthly*, under both Holland and Gilder, was forthright in its criticism of social and political wrongs.

Holland brought other characteristics to his editorship that were perhaps less fortunate in their effect upon the magazine. He had almost no esthetic sense at all, believing that didactic intent was the only justification for literature. He was also a prude: he struck from a manuscript about mountain climbing a comparison of the shape of a mountain peak and a woman's bosom. On another occasion he objected to an illustration for a poem on a

woman's reverie while undressing, arguing that readers of the
magazine would suppose that the illustrator would have to be
present during the undressing, even though the illustration was of
the reverie, not the woman! [3]

Holland was not the only editor of the period with an over-
developed sense of propriety, nor was *Scribner's Monthly* the only
magazine to show the effects of editorial squeamishness. Holland
merely reflected the time he lived in, and his conservatism "not
only made him the acknowledged spokesman for the moralities of
the nation, but also helped to make him the most successful magazine editor of his time." Nearly twenty years after his death, when
the magazine-reading public had become far more tolerant, Gilder wrote that "There's nothing a publisher is more sensitive to
than the criticism of readers." [4] And, indeed, the hundreds of letters received by the editors of the magazine from irate readers
who found some article or story immoral prove that Holland's
concern over these matters was well founded.

If the appearance of the magazine reflected the character of its
editor, the history of the company reflects no less the character of
its business manager. Roswell Smith was an unusual combination
of financier, perfectionist, and man of God. A stern Presbyterian,
he had little use for people who made money for money's sake; his
own desire in life was to do great and good things, and he believed that God would see to it that all such efforts were also
commercially profitable.

To Smith belongs much of the credit for the magazine's commercial success. He instituted two policies that revolutionized
magazine publishing: pre-paid bulk mailing and inexpensive,
large scale advertising. Other magazines, notably *Harper's*, had included advertisements before *Scribner's Monthly* entered the
market, but *Harper's Monthly* in 1870 was charging $500 per page
for ordinary pages, $1000 per page for space next to reading mat-
ter. *Scribner's Monthly* charged $100 for an ordinary page, $200
for a page next to the magazine text. As a result, the volume of
advertising in the magazine increased from 88½ pages in the
fourth volume (May–October, 1872) to 143 pages in Volume XXII
(May–October, 1881); and *The Century*, at the height of its popularity, often carried as many as six hundred pages of advertising in
a single volume. Because of this constant growth in advertisement

income, the editors of the magazine could substantially increase their payments for contributions.

Smith never tried to influence the editorial policy of the magazine. From the first issue of *Scribner's Monthly,* Holland and later Gilder demanded complete independence from the magazine's business office. Smith did take an active interest in the editing of the magazine. His mind was fertile with new editorial as well as commercial ideas, but, as one of the editors wrote, he never forced them upon the staff, "having faith in his associates." [5] As a result, the editorial course of *Scribner's Monthly* ran more smoothly than was common among the magazines of the period. Smith could always be called upon to provide a commercial reason to back an editorial decision, but he never allowed financial considerations to influence editorial policy.

II *Of Magazines . . .*

All the advantages gained by *Scribner's Monthly* through its popular new editor and capable business manager were needed to survive in a highly competitive field. To be sure, magazine publishing was an expanding business; between 1865 and 1870 an average of one hundred magazines a year were founded in the United States. Circulation gains kept pace with this increase, and on the basis of the expanding American audience, a magazine beginning its life in 1870 seemed to have a healthy chance of success. But statistics do not tell the whole story, for there were many hidden dangers. Two giants, *Harper's Monthly* and *The Atlantic Monthly,* dominated the market while dozens of lesser publications struggled for a footing. *Harper's Monthly,* with the strength of the House of Harper behind it, had acquired by 1870 the widest circulation of any American magazine to that time. *The Atlantic Monthly* was never able to compete with *Harper's* for circulation, but was foremost in the country in terms of that intangible— prestige. A few other magazines were strong enough to challenge these two, but the great mass of periodicals either turned to special interests for support or subsisted on second-rate pirated material.

Even if the competition had not been so keen, magazine publishing depended upon the whim of the American reader, who could be quick to take offense at a magazine that engaged in controversy, flirted with immorality, neglected whatever region of the country he came from, or ignored his special interests. Holland flouted the first of these traditions by actively engaging in controversy, but he acceded to the second by avoiding any taint of immorality.

Regional interests were a problem to the editors throughout the magazine's lifetime. Most of the magazines of the period were accused of being regional in their outlook at some time or another, but none more often or more unjustly than *Scribner's Monthly* and its successor, *The Century*. When Edward King's "Great South" series appeared, people in the North accused Holland of being confederate in his inclinations; later features, notably Cable's two articles on the position of the Negro in the South, brought cries from southerners that Gilder was provoking antisouthern sympathies; some western writers found the magazine eastern in its orientation, and it is not impossible that some easterners felt the editors paid too much attention to the West! [6] The criticisms suggest that *Scribner's Monthly* was, in fact, a truly national magazine, printing very little that was not American in origin or content, and drawing its American material from every section of the country.

The fourth tradition, that a magazine must appeal to all its readers' interests, was also one that the editors attempted to follow. Holland announced in the first number that the magazine would be "intelligent on all living questions of morals and society," and that each number would "interest and instruct every member of every family" reading it.[7] By and large, his promise was kept. Ambitious special articles and series kept the magazine from giving the appearance of formula publication, but each issue consistently seemed well-balanced, including poetry, fiction, commentary and feature material on the arts, sciences, and technology, along with portions of public affairs, religion, education, and history.

Because of its intelligent editorial policy, the commercial changes instituted by Roswell Smith, the willingness of the editorial staff to seek good writing and the business office to pay for it, *Scribner's Monthly* flourished during its eleven years of publication in spite of the hazards. The magazine succeeded because it was progressive; it grew in every sense during those eleven years, and the principal reason for its growth was the gradual supplanting of Holland by Gilder.

From November, 1870, to November, 1881, Holland and Gilder shared the editorial work of *Scribner's Monthly* in such a way that it is almost impossible to define exactly the separate areas of their responsibility. The operation of the editorial offices of *Scribner's Monthly* was radically different from the operation of a similar magazine today. There were no distinct departments within the staff; no single editor was in charge of incoming manuscripts or of proof reading; there were no poetry editors or drama editors. All, as a later member of the ranks reported, did "whatever came into their hands." [8] There were, of course, individual situations in which one or another of the editors preferred to take responsibility; but the lines separating areas of responsibility constantly shifted and often disappeared.

Final responsibility for the magazine rested with Holland. During the early years of the magazine, his decision about what was to be printed in the magazine was irrevocable. Holland also set the editorial policy of the magazine, and he brooked no interference in this area. When, for example, Gilder gently protested some extreme opinions expressed by Holland in an editorial arguing against women's rights, Holland replied that, although he thanked Gilder for his "tenderness toward [him] and [his] reputation," he "could not consent to have any editorial connection with the magazine" if he "were to feel in the least curbed in the expression of [his] well-considered opinions" (GP, Sept. 18, 1870). Gilder necessarily gave in, although later he was more assertive in matters of editorial policy.

Just as Holland guarded his editorial control, Gilder asserted himself in the writing of "The Old Cabinet," his regular editorial contribution to *Scribner's Monthly*. The main instrument of editorial policy, "Topics of the Times," written exclusively by Holland, was confined to what Holland considered the most significant issues of the day—thereby excluding most of art and literature. Gilder devised "The Old Cabinet" as a more frothy vehicle of editorial comment, principally on art and esthetic matters. Holland objected several times to the department: art and literature, he felt, ought not to be discussed except in moral terms; and Gilder's essays, he feared, were of little interest to the subscribers. Gilder defended his contributions and won. Later he won another battle to be the only contributor to "The Old Cabinet," arguing that the department presented a peculiar editorial viewpoint that could not be duplicated by another writer (GP, Nov. 4 and 10, Dec. 19 and 24, 1870).

Gilder was never a "yes-man" for Holland editorially, but he did not have much to do with the tone of *Scribner's Monthly* during its first years. Holland set the editorial policy, requested most of the material, and accepted or rejected manuscripts. Gilder managed the magazine, did much of the editorial pruning and revision, watched for editorial and typographic consistency, and saw the magazine through the process of printing.

As the magazine became more firmly established, Holland gradually withdrew from direct editorial management in favor of Gilder. His withdrawal took two forms: first, an increasing acceptance of his young assistant's more esthetic point of view; second, a physical withdrawal from the offices of the magazine to his estate on the St. Lawrence. When the magazine was starting, he could answer Gilder's doubts concerning the literary value of George MacDonald's opening serial novel with the brusk assurance that "MacDonald will please *the people* as well as Bulwer or George Eliot" (GP, Sept. 9, 1870). His attitude underwent a gradual change as Gilder worked to broaden Holland's taste to include writings less moral and didactic in intent.

Holland apparently worked hard during the first three years of the magazine to establish it, but, beginning in 1874, he began to spend far more of his time away from New York. Three of his novels, *Arthur Bonniecastle, The Story of Sevenoaks,* and *Nicholas Minturn* appeared serially in *Scribner's Monthly* between 1873 and 1878; and the writing of these novels, plus his editorials for the magazine, must have occupied nearly all his time. His health was beginning to fail as well, and he was forced to turn over increasing editorial responsibility to Gilder, in whose capacity he had great faith. "I am proud of what you do" for the magazine, he wrote Gilder, banteringly, "Was I not infinitely acute in my choice [of an assistant editor]?" (GP, July, 1871).

The ascendancy of Gilder as editor-in-chief, in fact if not in name, was fortunate for the magazine at this time. While Holland's literary star was declining, Gilder's was rising. In 1869 and 1870 Holland was able to write to most of the literary figures of the time in an effort to get contributions for the new magazine;

but within a few years he was far out of step with the new generation of writers then becoming prominent, men and women who
were close friends of Gilder. William Dean Howells recounted an
incident when Holland listened to a discussion of literature for
over an hour, then said, as he got up to leave, "I have been listen-
ing to the conversation of these young men for over an hour. They
have been talking about books. And I have never before heard the
names of any of the authors they have mentioned." [9]

During the same period Gilder's home at 103 East 15th Street
was becoming a focal point for the most brilliant artistic and literary society in New York. On Friday evenings Gilder and his wife,
Helena DeKay Gilder, herself an accomplished artist, were "at
home" to such people as pianists Paderewski and Adele aus der
Ohe, violinist Leonora von Stosch, singer Clara Louise Kellogg,
and actors and actresses Salvini, Joseph Jefferson, Eleanora Duse,
and Helen Modjeska, not to mention literary figures like Mark
Twain, Bret Harte, Howells, James, and Cable. Gilder was very
much in the artistic and literary swim, as a magazine editor must
be.

Gilder's apprenticeship under Holland could not have lasted
more than three or four years. From about 1874 or 1875 Holland
became more of a contributor than an editor of *Scribner's
Monthly*, while Gilder took over almost complete editorial control. That the magazine did not suffer from the change is indicated by a comparison of the table of contents for any volume of
the magazine before 1873 with one of 1876 or later. The earlier
names include George MacDonald, Holland, Mrs. Oliphant, and
sundry forgotten theologians, leavened with such others as Edward Eggleston (who was the only early contributor for whom
Gilder was responsible), R. H. Stoddard, and Saxe Holm (Helen
Hunt Jackson). In 1876 the monthly was printing significant work
by Bret Harte, Thomas Wentworth Higginson, Thomas Bailey Aldrich, Sidney Lanier, William Cullen Bryant, Henry James, and
Ivan Turgenev. By the end of the decade the circulation was
over one hundred forty thousand, twenty-five thousand dollars
worth of manuscripts rested in the vault, the battle with *Harper's
Monthly* had been won (at least to the satisfaction of Gilder and
his staff), and Gilder was complaining that people he met in the
streets were carrying "concealed manuscripts" in an effort to get
into the best-paying, most influential magazine in the world. [10]

III *Birth of* The Century . . .

The extraordinary growth of *Scribner's Monthly* from 1870 to 1880 aggravated the fundamental separateness of Scribner and Company, the publishers of the magazine, and the parent book publishing house of Charles Scribner and Sons. The differences that grew up between the two firms reached a climax which in 1881 brought about a complete separation.

When Scribner and Company was formed, Charles Scribner was the least willing of the three partners to set up a new company to control the magazine; it was the insistence of Holland and Smith, along with Scribner's desire to have Holland as editor, that persuaded him to lend his name to the new magazine. He had controlled the company that had produced *Hours at Home*, but in the new venture he was only a minority stockholder with forty percent of the voting stock. Charles Scribner died less than a year after *Scribner's Monthly* was founded; and, though his sons Blair and Charles Scribner III were always interested in the success of the magazine, the relationship between the book firm and the magazine firm was further attenuated.

When a dispute arose in 1881 over the rights of the magazine firm to publish books serialized in the magazine, Roswell Smith and the Scribners agreed that the only solution was to dissolve the partnership, so Smith bought out the Scribner interest and set up a new company to publish the magazine, virtually unchanged in format, under a new name. Gilder suggested that the magazine take the name of the newly formed Century Club. In November, 1881, *The Century Illustrated Monthly Magazine* presented its first issue as Volume XXIII of a series that began with the first issue of *Scribner's Monthly;* only a note on the title page reminded the reader that it was Volume I of a "new series." In return for the change of name, the Scribners agreed not to publish another magazine with the name "Scribner" on the title page for five years from the date of the agreement. They followed the terms of the contract precisely; the first issue of *Scribner's Magazine* appeared in January, 1887.

In all of these changes Holland took no part. For nearly the last year of *Scribner's Monthly* he was too ill to participate in any of the affairs of the magazine. He lived long enough to see the first issue of *The Century* and died a few days later on October 12, 1881. Thus *The Century* gives the illusion of representing a complete break with the earlier magazine—new publishing company, new name, new editor-in-chief—and yet all three were virtually unchanged. The Century Company was just Scribner and Company centralized in the person of Roswell Smith; *The Century Magazine* was indistinguishable from *Scribner's Monthly* in all aspects except its name; and Gilder had been *de facto* editor of *Scribner's Monthly* for five or six years before he acquired the title. The events of 1881 do not represent disruptive changes at all, but are simply a recognition of an evolution that had been taking place for years.

The offices of Scribner and Company, publishers of *Scribner's Monthly*, were located in 1880 at 743 Broadway, third floor back, in a building with the Scribner bookstore, which occupied more sumptuous quarters on the main floor. There was no elevator, and the two long flights of stairs and the dingy hall connecting the offices were discouraging. The Century Company, publishers of *The Century Illustrated Monthly Magazine*, occupied the entire fifth floor of a new building in Union Square, with an elevator and broad, airy halls. The offices were covered with rich oriental rugs, lighted by windows of studio proportions, and decorated with original art works. The change in surroundings symbolizes the change in character of the magazine. *Scribner's Monthly* fought for its existence against the forces of the established monthlies, *Harper's* and *The Atlantic; The Century*, from its first issue, had circulation and prestige equal to its competitors'. In 1870, Gilder noted, the editors were forced to beat the bushes for printable articles and stories; in 1881, they were deluged with many times what they could possibly print. Nor did *The Century* stop growing. Only six years after its founding, *The Century* came to possess "the largest audience that was ever gathered about any periodical of its class printed in the English language." [11]

Many factors contributed to the rapid rise of the magazine, not the least of them its organization. Roswell Smith provided nearly the best possible environment for creative and commercially successful work. He hired youthful, energetic men and saw to it that they became closely involved with the success of the magazine. Each of the editors under Gilder—his associate editor, Robert Underwood Johnson; assistant editors C. C. Buel, L. Frank Tooker,

William Carey, and Sophie Bledsoe Herrick; and art editor, Alex-
ander William Drake—was a writer of merit as well as a capable
editor. It is a testimony to Gilder's powers of administration that
there were only rare and isolated incidents of bad feelings among
his virtuosi.

But Gilder's function was never overwhelmingly administrative.
For the entire thirty-nine years during which he edited *Scribner's
Monthly* and *The Century*, he never lost contact with the fruits of
his editing, the magazine itself. Each issue of *The Century* con-
tained about one hundred and fifty thousand words by thirty to
forty contributors, and Gilder felt that every word was his responsibility. Much of the responsibility was delegated. Gilder "had too
many other duties to permit him to spend much time and strength
on so prosaic and benumbing a task as the painstaking perusal of
proof," [12] but he read every issue of the magazine carefully enough
to keep his subordinates from becoming remiss in their typographical examination.

Although Gilder's particular responsibilities for the magazine
were at the highest level—cultivating new contributors and keeping the old—he was responsible for several of *The Century's* policies at the lowest level. *The Century* notified writers on receipt of
their manuscripts (a policy not followed by all magazines even
today), paid on acceptance, and returned rejected manuscripts in
plain envelopes, even to contributors who had neglected to en-
close postage. Bill Nye wrote that Gilder "could return rejected
manuscripts in such a gentle and caressing way that the disap-
pointed scribblers came to him from hundreds of miles away to
thank him for his kindness and stay to dinner with him!" But Gilder could also be unsparing in his criticism when talented writers
submitted inferior work.[13]

From the beginning of his career, Gilder was aware of the immense responsibilities of the most important element of editing a
magazine, the acceptance or rejection of manuscripts. In 1875 he
expressed his fears concerning an editor's obligations in a poem
that, for all its lightness of tone, echoes many of the comments of
disgruntled contributors:

> When I am dead and buried, then
> There will be groaning among men.
> I hear one sighing thus, "Alack!

> How oft he sent my poems back."
> And one, "He was too sensitive
> To take the essays I could give."
> Another, weeping, "Ah, how few
> Of my poor stories seemed to do."
> "I met him only once, and yet,
> I think I never will forget
> The way in which he said to me
> 'We're loaded down with poetry'."
> "In fact," said one, "There is no doubt
> That contributions wore him out." [14]

Six years later, when he became editor-in-chief of *The Century,* Gilder noted, again with some levity, that editors were more likely to gain enemies than friends (GL, Oct. 22, 1881). By 1896, however, he no longer joked about editorial pressures. "The care of manuscripts is the care of literature," he wrote then: "An editor's Hell is paved with rejected manuscripts which he wishes he had accepted. . . . Nowadays [he] is apt to get into a sort of panic before each new manuscript. In this mood he is more in danger of coddling the commonplace than of neglecting genius." [15]

Gilder did "coddle the commonplace." Certainly *The Century* published its share of commonplace verse and prose in the years to 1909. Gilder also "neglected genius," rejecting many stories and poems in which he recognized—too late—true talent. The point is that Gilder was always *aware* of his editorial obligation for "the care of literature." And, considering the pressures under which the magazine was published, the quantities of manuscripts submitted, and the mediocrity of the great majority of writers of the period, Gilder was as good as any editor has ever been at picking out consistently high-quality writing. Of the best American writers of the last two decades of the nineteenth century, three stand out far above the others—Howells, Twain, and James—and *The Century* published some of the best work of all three. Gilder was just as perceptive of the worth of the lesser writers of the period, for he published works by Bret Harte, Joaquin Miller, and Hamlin Garland among the Western writers; southern writers like George Washington Cable, Thomas Nelson Page, and Joel Chandler Harris; and poetry by Walt Whitman, Edwin Arlington Robinson, and, posthumously, Herman Melville. To be sure, these names are culled from a list of contributors numbering in the thousands, for

Gilder took pride in the fact that his magazine led all the others in the number of writers it introduced to the public.

He was just as proud of, but more troubled by, the great quantities of manuscripts sent to the magazine, quantities so large that backlogs of material were inevitable. In 1885 Gilder wrote a contributor that he did not want to look at his manuscript if there was any chance that he might want to accept it for the magazine: "the best way . . . of killing an article for a generation is to have it accepted by the Century Magazine" (GL, Feb. 13, 1885). In 1892 a contributor bought back an article from the magazine, explaining that he did not care to write "for the sepulchre." [16] In 1890, the magazine was receiving forty-five hundred manuscripts a year, of which it could print only four hundred; by 1905, the number of manuscripts had more than doubled while the capacity of the magazine remained unchanged.

Unfortunately, quantity of manuscripts has never necessarily produced quality. One of the editors of *The Century* described in this way his own awakening to the facts of life as they apply to magazine publishing: "I had thought that [manuscript reading] . . . would be a simple matter: it was merely a question of being greatly delighted or intolerably bored. The great mass of contributions that lay between these two extremes . . . did not enter into my naïve calculation at all." [17] To a magazine editor with limited space at his disposal and twelve deadlines each year, the choice is almost never between "good" and "bad," but, at best, between "good" and "better," and, at worst, between "bad" and "not so bad." Editors are often forced to purchase mediocre manuscripts because nothing better is immediately in sight, and to refuse very good manuscripts because the vault happens to be full of manuscripts previously accepted.

Gilder's work was made more difficult by the necessity to plan the magazine months in advance. A prospectus was issued before each new volume, sketching out the contents of the magazine for the following half year. On occasion, timely material might be inserted in a volume, forcing out other articles and stories that had been advertised and swelling the contents of the vault. Human frailties among *The Century's* contributors produced additional complications. Gilder often had to plead with authors who had contracted for stories and articles which were advertised and then were late arriving. Serials presented an even greater problem. Once a serial was advertised and begun, the editors lived in dread of any of three calamities: that the author might be unable to present copy in time for an installment, that he might lengthen his work beyond what the editors had planned for, and, worst of all, that he might introduce "unsuitable" material into his plot. In the first situation the editors could thin out installments in hand; in the second, other material could be held back; but, in the third, should the author prove intractable, Gilder could do nothing but wait for the letters of protest to arrive from his readers.

In his first year as editor of *The Century* Gilder experienced a difficult encounter with an "unsuitable" serial. Frances Hodgson Burnett's *Through One Administration* is, to the modern reader, scarcely more morally objectionable than her most famous story, *Little Lord Fauntleroy*. The novel develops a theme of the love of Tredennis, an army officer of simple character and rather dog-like devotion (not unlike that of Captain Dobbin of *Vanity Fair*), for Mrs. Bertha Herrick Amory. Tredennis falls in love with her while she is single, but is forced to leave for duty on the western frontier. When he returns to Washington society, he finds her not too happily married. The plot skirts the edge of adultery, providing a moral ending only in the last chapters. To many of the readers of *The Century*, however, Tredennis' fatal fascination for a married woman, though the situation is kept technically within moral bounds, was intolerable. When the letters bearing what Gilder called "the only serious, dangerous, and at the same time correct criticism" he had ever received as an editor began pouring in, Gilder attempted to persuade Mrs. Burnett to make some changes. She refused, and the angry letters to the editor and adverse newspaper criticism gave Gilder what he called the greatest "set-back" he had experienced as an editor (GL, Feb. 6, 1883).

Here, it would seem, is evidence of the "genteel tradition" in full bloom. Here is the timid editor recoiling from a "few" letters of protest from hypersensitive readers and inflicting his own caution on a writer who might otherwise have chosen and developed significant human themes. But any editor of the period would have reacted in the same way. The great magazines of the period from 1870 to 1900—*The Atlantic, Harper's, The Century,* and *Scribner's*—were a conservative force. With large financial investments, commitments to their subscribers, and conservative traditions stretching back to their founding, the magazines resisted changes in the tone or style of what they printed when the changes seemed to threaten their investments, their commitments, their traditions.

The situation was unfortunately restrictive to the writers. The magazines had grown so rich that payments for serial rights to a novel published in *The Century* or *Harper's* were in some cases greater than royalties from book sales. Writers were tempted to direct their efforts toward magazine publication to obtain maximum income. Though they knew in advance (or quickly found out) what that option demanded in their choice of theme, situation, and language, the economic rewards were great, and many writers confined their efforts at changing the situation to railing at the editors' right to print what they wanted in their own magazines. One can sympathize with the writers, but one can hardly agree with them. The situation has always existed and always will; whatever market for literature is most prosperous will always be the most conservative, whether it is the family magazines of the 1890's or network television of the 1960's. True pioneers in literature will take their experimental work elsewhere.

If the magazine's conservative position is granted, what then can serve as a criterion for judgment of an editor's liberalism within this necessarily conservative framework? Gilder himself described the editor's responsibility in these terms, in a letter of May 29, 1883, to Henry James: "It requires the greatest skill . . . to know just how far it is in good taste and good faith to go in the matter of opposing the convictions and shocking the prejudice of the readers for whom you edit. My own idea is always to be a good way in advance of the multitude and to insist upon the literary view and upon a decided freedom of discussion" (GP). In other words, the liberal editor must recognize two responsibilities: one to contributors who challenge the standards of ethics and esthetics, and one to the readers of his magazine who, in T. S. Eliot's words, "cannot bear too much reality." The two are in constant opposition. Every manuscript that arrived in Gilder's office presented the possibility of a new decision between these two forces. More often than not, as we shall see, his decision was for the challenge and against the standards of his own day.

CHAPTER 2

Poet-Editor, Editor-Poet

I *The Editor as Poet*

WRITING in 1905 in answer to a question about what honors he had received, Gilder listed his honorary degrees from Harvard, Princeton, Yale, and Wesleyan, his fellowships and memberships in sundry societies, and then added, "I dare say I am various other things that I cannot remember, but if you can state on positive evidence that I am a poet, I would rather that than all the rest put together" (*LRWG*, 367–8). The relative importance of Gilder's activities is clear to anyone who studies him: he was first of all an editor, and second a poet. His avocation may have influenced his editorial policy, but it was clearly subordinate to it. Nevertheless, a phenomenal amount of his energy and time went into the composition of verse that is almost entirely forgotten today, but that demands attention in this study. To understand Gilder the editor, it is necessary to understand Gilder the poet.

Writing poetry was, in many ways, more than an avocation for Gilder. In a letter to Edmund Clarence Stedman in 1892, he declared, "I feel as the years go on that so long as I have the poetic impulse, and so long as work in that direction seems to be not entirely thrown away, I ought to treasure all available time and energy for original work." [1] It is appropriate and only too natural that such a statement should have been directed to Stedman, for it was he, more than anyone else, who was Gilder's "master" in the writing of poetry. Stedman was eleven years older than Gilder and by the time of their first meeting in 1868 or 1869 was already established as a publishing poet. Stedman was also Gilder's closest friend throughout his life and certainly the most devoted supporter and critic of his poetic efforts. On the whole, however, Stedman's poetry probably influenced Gilder very slightly.

But, although Gilder rarely imitated Stedman's technique in

[31]

verse, he was certainly influenced by the criticism of his friend; and in many ways the history of Gilder's development as a poet is the history of their friendship. Stedman was interested in Gilder's progress from the first and Gilder was guided by his friend. "I closely follow your literary growth and career and especially your growth as a poet," Stedman wrote Gilder, "for you interested me years ago in Newark and almost seem to me like a younger brother. . . . Let me assist you in all your flowering etc. when you are ready to 'come out,' and review you besides" (GP, Aug. 19, 1873).

Gilder, twenty-nine years old and just beginning to grope for a poetic style, needed help to crystallize the vague feelings he had about poetry. Here, for example, is his anguished cry to Stedman over the poetic phenomenon summed up in Pope's lines, that "True wit is wisdom to advantage dress'd,/What oft was thought but ne'er so well expressed": "There is one thing that worries me a little. As I dip into Chaucer and Mrs. Browning . . . parts that I know I never saw before, I find the same thought sometimes, though of course differently expressed. I know that every line comes out of my very soul, but will the world believe that?" Or, again, he expresses the long, long thought of youth: "I mean to make my first book . . . perhaps as careful a study as has ever been made of the subject of which I told you [the discovery of young love in two persons]. And then I shall turn to study, study, for years for the calmer philosophic work of maturity."

Or, finally, here is his statement of youthful egotism:

> I have read really very little of sonnet writing, but so far as I have read I have seen nothing to convince me that mine—that is my first poem—might for instance cover more ground than Shakespeare's and avoid the things that are not fine in his. Since conceiving my own poem I have read Dante's "New Life." Now in quality I might never touch either Shakespeare or Dante, but I am a blunderer if I do not make something in *some respects* finer than either. You will not misunderstand me. One's aim should be high—Better, (for me at least) fail in a great thing than succeed with a little.[2]

It would probably be improper to quote these youthful admissions were it not for the responses they provoked from Stedman. Here, clearly, was a young voice needing only to be told to rebel against the commonplace and to seek his own idiom—to study, perhaps, but also to gain wide experience and reflect that experience as directly and precisely as possible. Stedman was not the man to give that advice. Instead he wrote, on September 16, 1873, "what I am particularly gratified with, is that you are rejecting now the oddity and obscurity I have sometimes 'cried out' at with regard to some of your verse" (GP). Criticizing one poem on February 4, 1874, he let his own prejudices influence him in this criticism of Gilder's style: " 'The Vision' seems to me too 'fleshly,' and too Swinburnian, with a dash of Morris besides" (GP).

Finally, if Gilder had any doubts as to whether he wrote for himself or for the reviewers, these words of Stedman's on October 28, 1875, must have settled the question for him: "I must congratulate you heartily upon the deserved success of your 'New Day.' I certainly don't remember any first book of poetry which has had so extended notice—Miller's excepted, and he had a European endorsement. . . . Of course you must expect some rude criticism. But you certainly are not being overlooked—and have made an impression" (GP). Gilder would perhaps never have been a great, even a very good poet, under the most ideal circumstances. But surely his coming under the influence of such a vocal, friendly, and poetically mediocre tutelage as Stedman's must have damned his chances eternally.

By about 1875 whatever damage Stedman could inflict upon him was done. From that date on there is a subtle difference in the correspondence between Gilder and Stedman. *Scribner's Monthly* had risen to a position of prestige among the country's magazines: and, with its rise, Gilder had become an editor of prominence. Beginning in 1875 every letter of Stedman's criticizing Gilder's poetry might be balanced with one from Gilder criticizing Stedman's—and exercising the editor's prerogative of insisting upon the changes recommended if the poem were to be printed. With the withdrawal of Holland from most of the editorial duties of the magazine, Gilder became something of an *arbiter elegantiae* of the nation's scribblers in verse. Had he not learned about respectable mediocrity in verse from Stedman, he soon would have from the quantities of poems poured onto his editorial desk. Here again was a condition under which only the hardiest of poetic geniuses could bloom. To read hundreds, sometimes thousands, of verses each year by writers, mostly female, whose ideal of poetry was to "get into *The Century*" would tax the resources of even the greatest poet. If Gilder had any lingering ideas of writing for a generation beyond his own, of not merely seeking popularity, his forty years of editing would have conditioned him to the lesser goal.

Small wonder then that his poems are mostly forgotten today, and small wonder that in his own day he was one of the most popular poets in America. One indication of his popularity is the number of his poems that were set to music—no less than fourteen set with his permission, and there were doubtless others, pirated by less scrupulous publishers. He was represented prominently in most anthologies of the period, and his volumes of poetry went through many editions. *The New Day* was published in four editions between 1875 and 1887, several requiring more than one printing. *The Poet and His Master,* first published in 1878, was reprinted twice, in 1885 and 1887. His first gathering of his works to 1894, *Five Books of Song,* had four editions between 1894 and 1900. Then, in 1908, Gilder was chosen as the first living poet in a projected series by Houghton Mifflin of "American Household Poets." The prospect of a volume of Gilder's poems among the pots and pans, as it were, may be ironic now; but in 1908 it was a singular honor to be chosen for a series that was to include Bryant, Longfellow, Lowell, and Whittier.

In nearly all their comments, Gilder's contemporaries accepted his poetry uncritically as the outpouring of genius. Two such comments, widely separated in time and in their author's knowledge of poetry, will suffice. In 1877 John Burroughs wrote Gilder, jocularly referring to a poem that had recently appeared in *Scribner's Monthly,* "if you go on writing in this way you will have to be looked after. Most of your things have a permanent value as literature and you will soon have to sort them out and put them in a volume" (GP, Jan. 23, 1877). Edwin Arlington Robinson, writing near the end of Gilder's life, is more complimentary:

> Putting aside the past-mastery of technique—the praise of which at this late date would be banal—I admire most your willingness to look life in the face without resorting to the nauseating evasions of the uncompromising "optimist." The predominance of this willingness to be honest . . . is to my mind the most admirable thing in life or art. . . . To be more concrete I will say I

have long thought Non Sine Dolore not only interesting but exciting—and this is only one poem of thirty or forty of which I could say as much.[3]

Between these two letters are hundreds of others, overwhelmingly complimentary and, in the authors' views, asserting Gilder's permanent place in literature.

Gilder took the writing of poetry very seriously. The three comments to Stedman we have quoted are typical of his earliest gropings toward an understanding of the nature of poetry. Not long after those youthful letters he must have given up the quest, for in his later writings on poetry he is no longer attempting to distill that ineffable, poetry, from thought; he became instead a formalist, considering himself something of an expert on the construction of the sonnet and the irregular ode. This change was probably also a function of his editorial work. Certainly Gilder could appreciate poetic genius when it was offered to him for publication. More often, however, he was forced to lower his aim to the recognition of proper scansion and true rhyme. His letterbooks are full of suggestions for emendations of limping meters and off-rhymes. He applied the same rules for form in poetry to his own work to such an extent that it is hard to find a line of his poetry that is metrically bad and almost impossible to find a rhyme that is not perfect.

Taken as a whole, Gilder's poetry belongs to that large school of poets, situated generally in the great cities of the Northeast during the last two decades of the nineteenth century, who believed that it was the function of poetry to show man the way to the ideal in life. With Gilder in the school were Stedman, Thomas Bailey Aldrich, Edwin Markham, Robert Underwood Johnson, and many others. Yet in some ways Gilder was not quite in step with the other poets of the school. In the first place, his poetry had a broader range. While a fairly large number of his poems are lyrics which are patently derivative, mostly from the early romantics, these poems are concentrated in his most youthful works and his last works, chiefly in *The New Day*, published when he was not yet thirty, and in *In Helena's Garden*, published just a few years before he died. Among the poems written between these two volumes, the percentage of vigorous verse is not unimpressive, especially when one considers how much of it is "occasional verse."

However tentatively, he did attack current abuses as he saw them, as in "Congress: 1878," which he compared to "a sound like jackals ravening to and fro," or "The Whisperers," a criticism of "secret deals" in politics. "The Whisperers" is based upon a single metaphor—the whisper is a shout of warning—and the implications of it work out for Gilder rather well:

> They who once conversed so quietly, secretly, with shrugs and
>   winks and finger laid beside nose—what has happened to
>   their throats?
> For speak they never so low, their voices are as the voices of
>   trumpets; whisper they never so close, their words are like
>   alarm bells rung in the night
>
>   . . . .
>
> And the people listen with bowed heads, wondering and in grief
>
>   . . . .
>
> And thieves, lurking in dark places and furtively seizing that
>   which is not their own; and the petty and cowardly briber,
>   and he who is bribed, nudge one another;
> And the anarch and the thrower of bombs clap hands together,
>   and cry out: "Behold these our allies!"
>   (*Poems*, 402–3)

As "The Whisperers" suggests, Gilder also did some experimenting with free-verse forms, probably most successfully in "A Lament for the Dead of the Jeannette Brought Home on the Frisia." But, for all his admiration of Whitman (which is discussed later in this chapter), Gilder sensed his failure to master Whitman's technique, and free verse is rare in his writings. In a sense, he was obsessed with form in poetry and was intelligent enough to recognize that Whitman's poems had form—a perception quite beyond that of most of his contemporaries. But, for the most part, he was content to work in the old forms. He wrote ballads, like "John Carman," which tells of an idiot shoemaker who, "consoled" in his grief by a minister who prates of God's love, sets fire to the church:

> "You say it was He who killed her"
> (His voice had a fearful sound):

> "I'd have you know, who love him so,
> I've burned His house to the ground."
> (*Poems*, 105)

His sonnets, a most favored form, include some of Gilder's best and worst work. Most often they call up echoes of Keats and Shelley that overpower any possibility of originality on Gilder's part, but on occasion Gilder could manage something—not exactly *new*, but perceptive and, finally, poetic, as in his sonnet on the sonnet:

> What is a sonnet? 'T is the pearly shell
> > That murmurs of the far-off murmuring sea;
> > A precious jewel carved most curiously;
> > It is a little picture painted well.
> What is a sonnet? 'T is the tear that fell
> > From a great poet's hidden ecstasy;
> > A two-edged sword, a star, a song—ah me!
> > Sometimes a heavy-tolling funeral bell.
> This was the flame that shook with Dante's breath;
> > The solemn organ whereon Milton played,
> > And the clear glass where Shakespeare's shadow falls:
> A sea like this—beware who ventureth!
> > For like a fiord the narrow floor is laid
> > Mid-ocean deep sheer to the mountain walls.
> > (*Poems*, 134)

Perhaps this one poem, ranging from the sheer bathos of the "ah me!" of line seven to the quite effective simile of the last two lines, will stand as an illustrative example for the bulk of Gilder's poetry. Rare is the poem written by him that has not some poetic intelligence in it; equally rare is the poem that carries itself to completion unscathed.

Gilder lived at a time when a most unfortunately gutless poetic diction was the rule for all but a handful of poets, at least in America. Gilder's prime concern was with ideas—not, as the great, even good poet's must be, with *words*. In this respect he was again like his colleagues in the idealist school, but his ideas were inclined to be a little more tough-minded than were most of theirs. Optimism is common in Gilder's poetry, but it is balanced by a Calvinistic realism that somehow suggests that his esthetic optimism, his sense that beauty somehow sets all right again, is, after all, only a sugar-coating to the pill of man's fate. He is, in short, a dualist, and lurking in even his most flowery lyrics there is often a sting of *memento mori,* that in life we are in midst of death. His most mature poetry is surely to be found in the collection *Two Worlds,* published in 1891 at the height of his career. The title poem for the collection consists of two paired verses:

I—THE VENUS OF MILO
Grace, majesty, and the calm bliss of life;
    No conscious war 'twixt human will and duty;
Here breathes, forever free from pain and strife,
    The old, untroubled pagan world of beauty.

II—MICHAEL ANGELO'S SLAVE
Of life, of death the mystery and woe,
    Witness in this mute, carven stone the whole.
That suffering smile were never fashioned so
    Before the world had wakened to a soul.
                                                    (*Poems,* 145)

Imperfect as these two verses are in terms of their abstractions—like "calm bliss of life"—and their poetic diction—like " 'twixt," and "mute, carven stone," the *idea* behind them is subtle and intelligent and certainly not to be sneered at as mere esthetic optimism.

Such other poems as "Hide Not Thy Heart" and "Non Sine Dolore" accept a Hell of everlasting pain and posit a painful life and even more painful hereafter. We have, for example, the following lines: "No life without a pang! It were not life/If ended were the strife—/Man were not man, nor God were truly God!" (*Poems,* 183–4). Although he had a deep-seated love for the Christian symbols, Gilder was an agnostic, and, to be sure, in his best spiritual poems he is quite unorthodox in his view of God. When he writes of God and faith, such concepts are used almost entirely for their non-literate, symbolic values, in a synthesis of rationalism and Platonism, as in these lines from "In Palestine."

He were a coward who should fear to lose
A blind, hereditary, thoughtless faith—

> Comfort of fearful minds, a straw to catch at
> On the deep-gulfed and tempest driven sea.
>
> Full well I know how shallow spirits lack
> The essence, flinging from them but the form.
> I have seen souls lead barren lives and curst,—
> Bereft of light, and all the grace of life,—
> Because for them the inner truth was lost
> In the frail symbol—hated, shattered, spurned.
>
> But faith that lives forever is not bound
> To any outward semblance, any scheme
> Fine wrought of human wonder, or self-love,
> Or the base fear of never-ending pain.
> True faith doth face the blackness of despair,
> Blank faithlessness itself; bravely it holds
> To duty unrewarded and unshared;
> It loves where all is loveless; it endures
> In the long passion of the soul for God.
>
> *(Poems, 239–40)*

Together with his philosophic dualism, Gilder had a greater interest in the techniques of poetry (beyond meter and rhyme) than most of his friends. When Lawrence Gilman sent him a copy of his *The Music of Tomorrow* (1907), which treats the music of Debussy as a kind of mood-poetry, Gilder was moved to write an extensive argument on the need for subordination of mood to action in poetry.

> I contend that the literary part of "mood" comes to me not more poignantly from the *specialists* than from those to whom the mood is not the perpetual method. That is,—while I am under the spell often—speaking of poetry—of the specialist in moods—like Poe we will say, nevertheless the poet of mood who is also the poet of action seems to me the greater artist. Shelley (Sensitive Plant, etc.), or Browning (Childe Roland), greater than Poe—Shakespeare or Keats greater than Verlaine or Yeats, as beautiful as the latter may be. (GL, Dec. 2, 1908)

His technical theories of poetry are backed by his editorial choices. Whenever the opportunity arose, Gilder chose more vigorous poetry than anyone in the ideal school could write. The opportunity, unfortunately, did not arise very often.

In short, Gilder's poetry is often not nearly so bad as the critics have assumed. Narrative poems like "John Carman" have a good deal of strength in the description of character; meditative poems like "Non Sine Dolore" present a viewpoint that was fresh in the nineteenth century and is not really shopworn today; all of his poems show a proficiency that, on occasion, escapes from being an obsession with technicalities and becomes a real technique. While his lyrics are sometimes indistinguishable from those of thousands of other versifiers of his day, his light verse is always deft. For example, a poet who can produce a monosyllabic gem like the following must command respect:

> "No, no," she said
> "I may not wed;
> If say I must—*nay* must I say;
> I cannot stay;
> Nay, nay, I needs must flout thee!"
>
> He turned about;
> His life went out;
> "If go I must, so must I go!"
> Cried she—"No, no;
> Ah, what were life without thee!"
>   (*Poems*, 262–3)

But a true evaluation of his poetry is almost as impossible today as it was when he was living and working. Since Gilder's poetry was so overrated then, modern critics (those who have bothered to consider it) have quite naturally reacted against all his verse, feeling there is no need to praise any of it. In 1901 James Onderdonk could write thus extravagantly of Gilder's poetry:

An echo of Dantean mysticism . . . may be discerned in the writings of a New York poet, who is still in perfect accord with his age. . . . It is not surprising that he should be misunderstood, or, except by a few, not understood at all. He wanders in the highest realms of spiritual poetry, whither in these days not many care to follow. When he descends to solid earth he gives us lines full of force and masculine vigor. . . . Behind the veil of allegory that obscures his verse shines the spirit of beauty, pure and translucent. Devoutly religious, he discerns in the creative poet an inspiration to heroism, an insight that anticipates science, a

spark of divinity that creates worlds. . . . But he betrays neither
an undue sentimentalism nor an over wrought didacticism. It is
impossible that such strains should strike the popular fancy, and
the poet himself is probably content to be accepted by a few.[4]

Such flattery, and it is typical of what was written of Gilder's
verse during his lifetime, prompted a reaction from most later
critics, who chose either to ignore Gilder entirely or to dismiss
him with a sentence or two. An exception is Ludwig Lewisohn, who, in his *Expression In America* (1932) attacked Gilder
viciously as a typical poet of "the age of tin," corrupted by the
"genteel tradition." But even he used as his strongest argument
against Gilder's poetry not the poems themselves, chiefly, but "the
discrepancy between the quality of his work and his standing and
reputation." [5]

It is not the purpose of this study to attempt a re-evaluation of
Gilder's poetry; the great bulk of it is, and deserves to be, forgotten. It is important to remember, however, that at times Gilder
could write a strong poem, that he was something of a poetic
theorist, and that, as an editor, he could recognize merit in poetry
when he saw it. His understanding of poetic forms, his theory of
mood and action in poetry, and his use of symbols made him as
well qualified a judge of poetry as any editor of the period. And, if
the pages of *Scribner's Monthly* and *The Century* are littered with
rhyming lines spawned by thousands of nameless versifiers, it is
more the fault of the age than the editor.

II *The Poet as Editor*

The strongest indictment of Gilder as a reactionary editor of
poetry was made by Carlin T. Kindilien in his *American Poetry of
the Eighteen-Nineties* (1956). Kindilien lumped Gilder with all
the other editors of American magazines flourishing in the 1880's
and 1890's in a conspiracy to preserve the Victorian values in
poetry:

The liaison which the poetic idealists had established with editors
and publishers was an intimate one: the strength of the continuing
tradition of Victorian poetry was a result of the coordinated activities of the writers, editors, and publishers. Richard Watson Gilder
of *The Century* [and other editors of similar magazines] . . .

early served notice of their respect for the ideals of the genteel
tradition and the type of poetry their magazines might be expected to welcome. (24)

The criticism is, in general, a fair one. There certainly was a
"school" of poets in the Northeast closely allied to, and in many
cases identical with, the editors of the most influential magazines.
These poet-editors accepted each other's poetry, reviewed each
other's books, and formed various organizations as much for the
opportunity to interchange ideas as for their ostensible purpose—
for example, the International Copyright League or the Century
Club. The school was, essentially, reactionary. They looked back
with awe upon poets like Longfellow, Lowell, and Whittier.
When Gilder received a volume from Oliver Wendell Holmes in
return for one of his own poems, he thanked the older poet in
terms which are typical of his respect for the earlier generation as
a whole:

> You have made me a most unexpected and delightful return for
> my tributary volume. It is the duty of us "youngers" to pay tribute
> to Caesar—but Caesar is not called upon to pay tribute to us. Your
> gift, therefore, has a special value to me and I thank you from
> my heart.
>   I would ask you what was the secret of the perennial value and
> excellence of your metrical products if it were not, after all, an
> open secret. It is the young of our generation who seem halting
> and feeble, while you who are called "old" are scintillating with
> youthful activity—who are producing art work of never failing
> freshness and beauty. Long, my dear Dr., may your light shine as
> a guide to the feet and an illumination to the mind and breast of
> many. (GL, Dec. 14, 1885)

But, although he respected the older generation of American
poets, and fit all the other criteria Kindilien set up for this league
of poet-editors, Gilder was not inclined to keep *The Century's* columns closed to all but ideal poets. A glance through the index to
any of *The Century's* volumes proves that point. Among the
twenty to fifty names in the poetry section of any volume it is rare
to find more than four or five writers who are conspicuous members of the ideal school. Among the writers for "Bric-a-Brac" and
"In Lighter Vein," *The Century's* light verse columns, the percent-

age is even lower. That, of course, does not prove that Gilder did
not discriminate against all except ideal verse, and to be sure,
many poets who contributed only a poem or two to the magazine
wrote verses indistinguishable from Stedman's or Stoddard's. But
among the thousands of poets who contributed to *The Century,*
many were more realistic than idealistic in their treatment of life.
Sidney Lanier, J. A. Macon, and Irwin Russell in the South often
sent realistic verse sketches of poverty in their region, while Joaquin Miller and William Vaughan Moody described some parts of
the real life in the Midwest and West in their verses.

The proportion of vigorous poetry to ideal verse printed by
The Century was never high, however, and Gilder was certainly
aware of the imbalance. He knew he was publishing a parody of
The Century's verse index when he published this satire by R. K.
Munkittrick in 1890:

> 'T is Ever Thus,
> Ad Astra, De Profundis,
>   Keats, Bacchus, Sophocles;
> Ars Longa, Euthanasia
>   Spring, The Eumenides.
>
>   *   *   *
>
> Dum Vivimus, Vivamus,
>   Sleep, Palingenisis;
> Salvini, Sursum Corda,
>   At Mt. Desert, To Miss ————.
>
> These are part of the contents
>   Of "Violets of Song,"
> The first poetic volume
>   Of Susan Mary Strong.
>   (XLII, 800)

But, considering the situation of American poetry in the 1880's
and 1890's, the few good poets and the multitudes of mediocrities,
and considering that what passed for poetry at the time was extremely popular, it seems unfair to find fault with Gilder for making the best of a situation that he did not create. What critics of
his policy forget is that Gilder did recognize poetic talent that did
not fit the clichés of the idealist school. There were so few examples of such talent available during his period of editorship that

they have been largely forgotten, but in this study, having considered what was wrong with the poetry printed by Gilder, it is only fair that we now turn to his treatment of such poets as Herman Melville, Edwin Arlington Robinson, and Walt Whitman. Though they represent a small proportion of the poets published in *The Century*, a study of Gilder's relationship with Walt Whitman, for example, is certainly more important than his editing of Miss Susan Mary Strong.

III   *Melville and E. A. Robinson*

Gilder's publication of several of Melville's later poems, posthumously, partially made up for the neglect of Melville by magazine editors and publishers during the last years of his life. Gilder wrote immediately upon hearing of Melville's death to Elizabeth S. Melville, requesting something for publication as a memorial to her husband. In her reply she agreed to the reprinting of some selections from Melville's last, privately printed, volumes of verse, *John Marr and Other Sailors* and *Timoleon*, adding, "I do not know of any publication in which I should be more pleased to see his name" (CC, Nov. 23, 1891).

The memorial did not appear until May of the following year, so crowded was *The Century's* schedule. Five poems were presented, with a head and tail-piece of symbolically mournful cast and a preface by Arthur Stedman. The preface was, on the whole, unfortunate. Stedman seemed to accuse Melville of hiding his light under a bushel when he called him "an author whose vogue had temporarily subsided [at the time of his death], partly through his own self-seclusion." He mentioned none of Melville's later fiction, but he assured the readers that *Typee, Omoo,* and *Moby Dick* were "classics of American literature," and that "Melville's art of casting a glamour over scenes and incidents in the South Pacific, witnessed and experienced by himself, has not been exceeded even by Pierre Loti" (XLIV, 104–5).

The few poems of Edwin Arlington Robinson which appear in the later volumes of *The Century* are not conspicuous for any inate quality in comparison with much of the other verse appearing with them. As early as 1897 Robinson sent Gilder a volume of his poetry, a practice followed by many poets of the period. Gilder returned a note of acknowledgment and compliment, as was his custom for such gifts, varying hardly at all from others of the kind. He wrote, among other things, that he had found "much of it that tasted good, and I thought I would tell you so" (GL, Mar. 27, 1897). By 1905 the two men were on terms friendly enough to allow Robinson to write to Gilder, "I am sorry to hear from Mr. [R. U.] Johnson that you are . . . confined to your home with illness. I can only hope that this is not the result of reading my poetry." Shortly after that Gilder exercised some of his influence with Theodore Roosevelt to obtain for Robinson a position as consul in either Montreal or Mexico City. Robinson found it necessary to decline the offer, fearing that it would take up too much of his time; but he thanked Gilder for attempting to help him: "Even though nothing should come of it, I shall always remember this episode as one of those pleasant and unexpected things that come about as frequently as the Phoenix." [6]

On this friendly basis their relationship continued through Gilder's lifetime. Few of Robinson's poems appeared in *The Century*, and he, like all the other poets who wished to appear there, had to bend to Gilder's will in the matter of emendations. For one poem Gilder insisted on the change of one word before the poem could be accepted. Robinson agreed to the change and humbly returned the poem to Gilder, corrected, with the assurance, "please be very sure that there is no trace of obstinacy or egotism in my attitude and that I am very grateful for your explanation, whatever may be your decision [about accepting or rejecting the poem]" (CC, Aug. 2, 1909). While part of his attitude may be ascribed to his position as supplicant to a whimsical editor, part is also deference to a mature judgment.

IV *Walt Whitman*

Melville and Robinson, however, had very little to do with *The Century* and its editor. Other markets were open to them, other friendships were available, and no one could argue that Gilder alone recognized their merits as poets. The one significant poet of this period who was indebted more than any other to Gilder's liberality, and who found in Gilder not only a friend, but a friend who could be of important help in achieving an audience, was Walt Whitman.

When Gilder first became aware of Whitman's work is not

known. Whitman's first contact with *Scribner's Monthly* was with Holland, and it was an unfortunate one. Two poems that he had sent to Holland on the urging of a friend were, as Whitman described the incident, "not rejected mildly, noncommittedly, in the customary manner, but with a note of the most offensive character. . . . The note provoked me: I threw it into the fire. I was always sorry I destroyed it: had I been well I should not have done so: It was a good specimen insult for the historian." [7]

Holland and Whitman thoroughly hated each other. To Holland, Whitman was an "old wretch" whose writings were full of "smut" and who had not "enriched American literature with any such congruous material as will enter into it and become a portion of the common stock appropriated by the public taste or the public need. You might strike out of existence all he has written, and the world would not be consciously poorer. . . . His art is a monster or a bastard, and will have no progeny." [8]

Seven years after Holland died Whitman said of him: "Holland is a dead man—there's hardly anything of him left today," meaning his work had not survived him: "He had his strut and is passed on: he was a man of his time, not possessed of the slightest forereach. . . . The style of man . . . who can tell the difference between a dime and a fifty cent piece—but is useless for occasions of more serious moment" (*WWW*, I, 184).

After Holland's insulting refusal of Whitman's poems, the two men had no further dealings with each other, personally. But their paths continued to cross in several unusual ways. While Holland was still officially editor of *Scribner's Monthly*, although he had little to do with the publication of the magazine, Edmund Clarence Stedman, with Gilder's support, embarked on a series of articles on American poets to be printed in the magazine. Holland "very strongly objected" to Stedman's inclusion of Whitman in the series, but Stedman and Gilder convinced him that "no review of the *American poets* could *ignore* a man who made himself so much talked-of at home and abroad." Holland gave his grudging consent, and Whitman was included in the series.

Stedman predicted that the article, which he intended to be "judicial," would please neither side in the debate on Whitman. Writing to Gilder, he complained, "I expect it will get me into all sorts of hot water. Probably you cold-blooded editors will think it a good thing for the magazine if it does." Actually Stedman succeeded in pleasing both sides. Holland wrote of the article: "I have read Stedman's paper. His treatment of Whitman's indecency is excellent, and the old wretch can no longer defend it. Without any pleas for morality and purely on aesthetic grounds, he demolishes all the old man's defenses and leaves him without any apology for adhering to his early smut." [9]

On the other side, although a few of Whitman's more extreme admirers thought Stedman had done Whitman an injustice, Whitman himself acknowledged Stedman's appraisal to be a fair one:

> I remember at the time Stedman had that long piece in the Century he appeared to have caught the idea—I was told so, told by several—that I was mad [i.e., angry]. . . . I was always troubled over this rumor. Nothing could have more misrepresented me. I regarded the piece as thoroughly friendly, thoroughly courteous, thoroughly fair—if not more. . . . It had been free criticism and I never resent free criticism. . . . I am only too glad to be read and examined as Stedman has read and examined me. After a long experience with men who neither hoped for truth nor would see it, it was like daylight to meet with such treatment as Stedman accorded me. (*WWW*, II, 547–48)

The article, really quite a judicious appraisal of a contemporary writer, and a controversial writer at that, was the first serious and intelligent criticism of Whitman to appear in an important American magazine. In it Stedman succeeded in separating completely Whitman's ethics from his esthetics, in criticizing the poems only, not the man. The criticism itself shows evidence of an intelligent reading of the poems, particularly "When Lilacs Last in the Dooryard Bloom'd." This article is one of the best critical pieces that Stedman wrote, and Whitman appreciated it as such.

For several years before Stedman's article appeared, Gilder had been helping Whitman in another way. In the late 1870's Whitman had but few friends and probably even fewer social connections in New York City. His reputation, his dress, his unusual manners and mannerisms made him generally unwelcome in the literary circles of New York. At about that time, as he told Horace Traubel later, "when most everybody else in [the Gilders'] set was throwing me down they were nobly and unhesitatingly hospitable." After recounting a typical social snub he had received by a woman in New York, he continued, "Now the Gilders were with-

out pride and without shame—they just asked me along in the natural way. It was beautiful, beautiful. You know how at one time
the church was an asylum for fugitives—the church, God's right
arm, fending the innocent. I was such an innocent and the Gilders
took me in" (*WWW*, II, 119).

Whitman showed his appreciation of the Gilders' treatment of
him by sending them, in 1880, copies of the latest edition of
Leaves of Grass. The accompanying letter described the books as
a "testimony of my remembrance and affection to you both." A
few days later Mrs. Gilder replied with a letter that showed that
Gilder was doing his part in spreading Whitman's fame abroad:

> We read some of your poems to a group of people—artists, etc.—
> in London, who were all intensely interested and impressed. One,
> Alfred Hunt, the landscape painter, was much moved over some
> of the descriptions of nature, the mocking bird and the pine trees
> especially. Richard talked about you with William M. Rossetti,
> your good friend, and others, who all were anxious to hear from
> you. Richard is very desirous to know whether you got [i.e., re-
> ceived a copy of] some of your poems done into Provencal, by
> W. C. Bonaparte Wyse. Would you write a line of acknowledge-
> ment to the latter, to be forwarded by Richard? Mr. Wyse would
> value it very greatly.[10]

This friendly reply probably prompted Whitman to write to
Gilder about a legal problem that had troubled him for many
years. When Thayer and Eldridge, the publishers of one of the
early editions of *Leaves of Grass*, went bankrupt, Richard Worthington, another publisher, bought the plates of the book and
began a long career of publishing a pirated edition of it. The
problem was compounded by Whitman's acceptance of a small
royalty check, perhaps no more than seventy-five dollars, which
Worthington shrewdly sent Whitman and which Whitman naïvely
accepted. On November 26, 1880, Whitman sent Gilder a summary of the situation accompanied by this plea: "Haven't you
someone learn'd in Copyright law and its infractions that could
take the thing in hand? *Injunct* Worthington or something?"
Then, to make the problem more difficult, he added: "nothing
must be done involving heavy fees, as I couldn't pay them" (*GP*,
Nov. 26, 1880). Unfortunately, Whitman's position was untenable

because of the "royalty" he had received from Worthington and the suit was not carried further.

On June 2, 1883, a short notice appeared in "The Lounger," a column conducted by Gilder's sister, Jeannette, in *The Critic:* "Dr. Bucke opens the second part of his new volume on Walt Whitman with a poem by R. W. Gilder, called 'When the True Poet Comes.' The reader would naturally suppose that the poem referred to Whitman, but Mr. Gilder tells me that such is not the case. He had another poet in his mind in writing." Gilder wrote Whitman immediately after the notice appeared and apologized for any impression it made that "might look as if I were not a friend and admirer of the subject of the book." The verses had been quoted without his permission; and, when he was asked if they were indeed about Whitman, he had been forced to reply "No, they were published in the magazine some time ago and were suggested by another writer." Bucke resented what he considered Gilder's withdrawal of a commendation to Whitman, and accused him of "not having the courage of his convictions." Whitman, however, defended Gilder's action; and, in view of Gilder's well-known championship of Whitman, he must have been correct.[11]

In 1884 Gilder conceived another opportunity to help Whitman. With the "War Series" beginning to take over the pages of the magazine and the editors' imaginations, he suggested that Whitman might like to write a prose description of his work as a volunteer nurse for the Union armies. The piece, "Army Hospitals and Cases," was published in *The Century* four years later. Meanwhile, two other short poems by Whitman appeared in the magazine, "Father Taylor and Oratory" in February and "Twilight" in December, 1887. From 1887 on, Whitman appeared once a year in the magazine until 1891. His contributions were not extensive, but they are remarkable in that Gilder apparently accepted every contribution Whitman made to the magazine.

Just a few months before his death, Whitman commended Gilder's treatment of his contributions: "I have sent him my pieces, put my price on them, been paid that price: an important item enough even taken alone: but added to that, Gilder takes what I offer unhesitatingly, never interjecting a single word of petty criticism. . . . Do you realize that that is treatment no other magazine editor in America has accorded us?" (*WWW*, IV, 171).

Whitman's personal opinions about Gilder are well documented in his conversations with Horace Traubel. That Whitman liked Gilder personally is perhaps not too surprising in view of the editor's friendliness to him. That he could praise some of Gilder's poetry is surprising, however, particularly because it was so foreign to Whitman's own style of verse: "Some of the hard and fast penny-a-liners in the poetic field affect to despise Gilder: they are a poor lot—most all of them: Gilder has written some poems which will live out the lives of most of the second-class songs of his day: genuine fine pretty big stuff: some of it, almost free" (*WWW*, III, 241).

More often, however, his view of Gilder's poetry was more what we might expect: "[Gilder's] poetry is considerably better than the average. I have friends who see a great deal in Gilder's work. Yet after all it never escapes being average, only average—it partakes of the general character of the characterless poetry of the magazines—that of porcelain, fine china, dainty curtains, exquisite rugs—never a look of flowing rivers, waving trees, growing lillies, floating clouds" (*WWW*, I, 126-7). Whitman himself recognized that he was unable to appreciate Gilder's poems, that the subject matter and techniques were of no interest to him: "He is rich on the emotional side—approaches me that way. Gilder is essentially a troubador singer, realizing grace, music, prettiness. . . . As for me, that is just the thing in which I seem to take no particular interest" (*WWW*, II, 373).

Looking beyond Gilder's poetry, which he really could not help disliking, Whitman had a deep admiration for Gilder personally. Comparing him with R. M. Bucke, Whitman came to this summary of Gilder's character:

Bucke's great point—greatest point of all—is his wonderful frankness, candor, openness. Gilder always strikes me as a man of the same sort: not so virile as Doctor, but frank, open—a man to be every way counted upon. Gilder seems to be coming on: is a bigger man than he was—by far bigger than when I first knew him. He likes fine things a little too well—that's where he misses the mark: is a little too much concerned about lightness (deftness) of touch, delicatesse. Yet he is an ideal editor—he knows how to put two and two together any time without a mistake. (*WWW*, II, 485)

Gilder's admiration for Whitman was expressed many times during Whitman's lifetime, but never so well or so publicly as at Whitman's seventieth-birthday celebration on May 31, 1889, at Camden. At that dinner, Gilder sat at Whitman's right hand. His speech was supposed to be on American literature generally and Whitman's place in it, and he early mentioned that "bright" among the list of American poets "shines the name of Walt Whitman." But a large section of his speech was intended as a careful criticism of Whitman's work. As might be expected, Gilder began with the form of Whitman's poetry:

> I am a stickler for form in literature, and one thing that I admire in Walt Whitman is his magnificent form. It is one of the most remarkable things in all literature and one of the most individual. In its kind, and at its best, it is unapproachable. No one can imitate with success Whitman's peculiar style; those who have tried—men, women, and boys—have all failed. No one can do it but Walt Whitman. At the same time the substance of Whitman's poetry pours freely into any language and carries its flow of meaning and of passion into whatever language it flows.[12]

Then, after praising Whitman's war poetry particularly, Gilder went on to summarize his feelings about Whitman's dualism, his glorification of both the spiritual and the physical in life. Since Gilder was an idealist, we might expect him to condemn Whitman's feelings about physical life, but we would be wrong.

> Those who look through his poetry like Dr. Johnson's old woman, for the naughty words, and who really know nothing about it, think that he is a poet of only one phase of life; but where outside of the Bible is there a stronger sense of the spirit? Where is there a stronger passion for immortality? a stronger vision of the individuality of the soul, the quenchless human soul? It is because he covers both the flesh and the spirit that Whitman reaches some of the loftiest minds of our day. (38–9)

Gilder's feelings about Whitman did not really crystallize until several years after Whitman's death. Early in 1905, Horace Traubel sent to the offices of *The Century* the manuscript of the first volume of his *With Walt Whitman in Camden,* selections from

which were published in the magazine the following November.
"You can imagine the experience," Gilder wrote to a friend, of
reading over a manuscript in which he was mentioned prominently and not always favorably. "Here are his opinions of myself
(contempt of course for my art, but personal affection . . .). He
says my use of the word *art* affects him like a bad smell" (GL, Apr.
18, 1905). But there was no rancor in his letter to Traubel discussing the manuscript, in which he tried to sum up Whitman's contribution as "a life, a work, and real conviction behind the lines"
(GL [July, 1905]).

In the following years Gilder's feelings underwent some slight
changes, but remained substantially the same. Writing to Clara
Barrus, he commented that he did not "accept Whitman throughout," but that, in general, "he had a charming and kindly personal-
ity, and he wrote, it seemed to me, great poetry, or great lines,
whether they are strictly poetry or not. It always seemed to me
that they were, and there is something more than art in the form
of his language" (GL, Apr. 23, 1906).

Later, writing on October 21, 1906 to Bliss Perry, he summa-
rized his feelings toward Whitman in even more detail:

> It is strange that with all one's knowledge of his early inconti-
> nence, of his early and late money speculations, of his outrageous
> self-puffery—still my memory of the old man is of a lovely, affec-
> tionate, clean character. The good in him is more powerful than
> the bad, just as the good in his book is more powerful than the
> absurd, the pompous, the animality, and the poetical failure.

Whitman's poetic sensibility appealed to Gilder more than any
other side of him, as he explained to Perry:

> The fact is that the dear old man who stood holding my hand out-
> side of the church at Bryant's funeral is the one I love—not the
> self-conscious semi-hobo: and the poet that stirs, astonishes, thrills
> and uplifts me is not the ranting theorizer reagitating (in prosaic
> and sometimes comical verse) the Emersonian doctrine like a
> mad man; and stripping off his clothes in half animal and half-
> religious frenzy.

That Whitman's excesses troubled him is further shown by the
theorizing he went through to explain the phenomenon of Whitman to Perry:

For years I have been comforted by a new realization of the old
doctrine of the defect of the quality. The way I have often put it
is that—especially in our day—it is rare that a man makes a tremendous impression in any line without having vastly too much
of the thing that gives him his success. Whitman could not have
reacted so effectively from conventions and with such great artistic
results if he had not had a tremendous push—and this push simply sent him too far.

Then, in explaining in what ways Whitman went "too far," Gilder revealed his own Victorian limitations in poetry; and he
showed, beyond what was required of him as editor of a family
magazine, why his sympathy with Whitman had to be limited.

Whitman's preaching of the animal side of life was unnecessary.
Self-control is the only thing it is necessary to *preach*—(as in
Tennyson's great line).[13] Animals we all are. The repression and
rigidity of Puritanism have passed. They never could long domi-
nate any community. But we are always animals evolving into
balanced, responsible human beings. To preach letting loose to a
race of procreators is as useless as William James declares the
preaching of fighting to the survivors of battles and descendants
of warriors,—which we all are.

Feeling thus strongly about the error of philosophy underlying
most of Whitman's work, Gilder then seems to be inconsistent in
still finding most of Whitman's poetry great. His rationale for his
attitude transcends considerations of morality: "Men of letters as
well as men of action work most effectively on some theory. . . .
Whitman's philosophy was at fault; but it was his 'working hypothesis.' There is no reason, however, that others should accept
his 'working hypothesis.' That is the mistake of his 'hot little prophets' " (GP). Here is the argument of not throwing out the baby
with the bathwater; if Whitman's underlying purpose is fallacious
but his statement of it beautiful, then we may accept the statement and dismiss the philosophy. This attitude accounts perfectly
for Gilder's acceptance of Whitman's poetry and for his rejection
of all that it stood for, his love for the man himself and distaste for
his "hot little prophets." This attitude is all that we could expect
from a man of Gilder's tastes and background, and it accounts

completely for his unusual relationship with a poet most of whose work could not be printed in his magazine.

Whatever his reasons, Gilder was, of all the editors with whom Whitman had dealings, the most receptive to his work and the most personally friendly to him. Critics who find both Gilder's own poetry and his editorial policy regarding poetry reactionary apparently ignore his treatment of the one poet of his time who was a true pioneer in modern verse.[14]

CHAPTER 3

Southern Renaissance and Revolt

IT WAS almost by accident that *Scribner's Monthly* became the leading northern periodical in support of the southern literary renaissance which followed the Civil War. Founded after the war, the magazine escaped the onus of Abolitionism that fell upon *The Atlantic Monthly* and *Harper's*. A series of articles on "The Great South" by Edward King, which began in 1873 and ran for more than four hundred pages in the magazine during the following two years, made *Scribner's Monthly* the most popular northern magazine in the South. With popularity and subscriptions came contributions, and the magazine during the entire period of Gilder's editorship led all northern periodicals in publications by southern writers.

Gilder personally contributed a great deal to this southern renaissance. He provided writers from all parts of the South with the same kind of editorial assistance and literary judgment later supplied by Maxwell Perkins to Thomas Wolfe and F. Scott Fitzgerald. His aid to writers as various as Thomas Nelson Page, Joel Chandler Harris, and Irwin Russell, among many others, was no less necessary to the development of those men as writers than was that of Perkins to a later generation. Furthermore, Gilder promoted a theory of the rebirth of letters in the South which had several important implications. The ante-bellum South, he reasoned, could not produce significant literature because of slavery. "It is of the essence of literature," he wrote, "that it should be free. It must criticize life without reserve." Gilder argued that emancipation had freed southern literature as well as the Negro. Only after the South had given up its "peculiar institution" could its writers consider freely and honestly the problems of human relationships. Pre-Civil War writers, he believed, had either written polemics or had fallen back on an escapist's romanticism that was only "the second fiddle to Cooper's second fiddle of Scott." Thus

he promoted the self-respect of the new class of southern writers
by giving them a *raison d'être*.[1]

Partially in accordance with this theory, partially because of the
national character of *Scribner's Monthly* and *The Century*, Gilder
refused to accept manuscripts that defended slavery or that
showed in any way an "unreconstructed" attitude toward southern social problems. On the other hand, some modern critics have
accused Gilder of "tacitly accepting the southern writers' assump-
tion of the racial inferiority of the Negro and of the Negro's con-
tentment with his lot in a feudal society." [2] In some respects this
criticism is valid: Gilder published some short stories that presented a southern rationale of the racial question. But in terms of
his own beliefs and his preference in this area, he was clearly on
the side of civil liberties for the Negro race. Since so few southern
writers shared his personal feelings in this matter, Gilder was necessarily forced to compromise his own feelings.

These general remarks are borne out by an examination of the
relationships between Gilder and several of the southern writers
who published extensively in *Scribner's Monthly* and in *Century*.
By considering some of these relationships individually, we will
be able to discern in detail Gilder's editorial function in relation to
the new Southern literature.

I *Thomas Nelson Page*

Probably the least reconstructed of the southern writers exhibited on the pages of *Scribner's Monthly* and *The Century* was
Thomas Nelson Page. Page broke into *Scribner's Monthly* with a
dialect poem in April, 1877. He thereafter abandoned verse for
the comparative freedom of the short story, but his theme and
pattern, which were to prove highly successful, hardly varied
from that first contribution. Page wrote chiefly about only two
classes in the South: the rich, heroic planter and the ignorant but
faithful house servant. These two types, repeated with infinite var-
iations in nearly all of his stories, provided a vehicle for his nostal-
gic romances in vigorous local color and at the same time promoted his subtle but pervasive views on white supremacy.

His first and most famous story, "Marse Chan," was accepted by
Gilder in 1881 but did not appear until April, 1884. The delay was
probably caused by the editors' fears about printing such a long

story almost entirely in a Negro dialect. In 1881 printing such a story might have been a risky undertaking, but by 1884 the readers of *The Century* had been exposed to so many of Irwin Russell's poems and to so many stories and poems by Joel Chandler Harris in Negro dialect that Page's story was no longer extraordinary. The story was immediately successful, exhibiting as it did a command of plot and characterization superior to Harris's and a control of dialect nearly as good. Page was thenceforth a desired contributor to many northern magazines.

Shortly after the appearance of "Marse Chan," Robert Underwood Johnson met Page in Richmond and suggested that the theme of Lessing's "Minna von Barnhelm" could be adapted to the situation of the War between the States and turned into a short story that would aid in re-establishing "good feeling between the sections of our country." Page reacted quickly, and by March 31, 1885, had completed his second most famous story, "Meh Lady." He sent it up to Gilder, giving credit to Johnson for the idea; and be added that, although the story "deals with the female rebel element," he thought it would not wound anyone.[3] It was published in June, 1886.

Between the publication of these two stories, Page also published a third dialect story, "Unc' Edinburg's Drowndin'," in *Harper's* for January, 1886. During the month it appeared, he submitted a third story to Gilder which did not meet with the editor's approval. Gilder returned it with this comment of January 19, 1886:

> Your "Soldier of the Empire" is capital, but it has what seems to me a grave defect: there is no climax, therefore no story. It is too much like a story for a sketch, but as a story it lacks dramatic completeness such as all your other stories have had. But I think that with a little pondering you can easily remedy this defect. Without such remedying the story is a great disappointment. (PC)

Gilder then praised "Unc' Edinburg's Drowndin'," adding, "but stories like this and 'Marse Chan' and 'Meh Lady' hold you up to a high standard." He then asked Page to return "Soldier of the Empire" when he had "really made a story out of it."

This rejection was not Page's first setback. The letter he wrote Gilder about "Meh Lady" mentioned another story that he was carefully rewriting after submitting it to "a gentleman" who had criticized it in much the same terms that Gilder had used (PC, Mar. 31, 1885). Page, like many of the writers of the new South, had limited self-critical abilities. His stories, when first submitted to the various magazines he wrote for, were often little more than sketches or were lacking in "portion and perspective," as one of his editors, Sophie B. Herrick, put it. Editorial pruning included the excision of incidents and details that reflected Page's anti-Negro, pro-Confederacy bias; but his attitude impregnated so much of his work that the reader could have no doubts about his feelings.

Page's earliest work is generally considered his best. After about 1887 he became more sentimental and romantic in his treatment of the old South, to the detriment of his strongest quality, the realistic portrayal of local characters. With the decline in his powers came a corresponding decline in his relations with Gilder and *The Century*. In 1886 Page wrote to Gilder asking for a contract to write a travel series while in Europe (PC, June 24, 1886). Gilder's lack of enthusiasm for the project was doubtless prompted by an understanding that Page's best work was in local color and that he could do nothing of great value away from the South. After gathering the best of his short stories in a volume (*In Ole Virginia*, [1887]), Page set to work on *Red Rock*, his first novel, which was not published until 1898.

In the process of writing *Red Rock*, Page engaged in a stratagem intended to pique editorial interest in the story. Soon after beginning the work, which he first thought of as a long story, Page wrote Gilder that he had inadvertently promised Scribner a "first shew" of the story after having previously promised it to *The Century* (PC, Mm. 28, 1887). He later again referred to Scribner's eagerness to see the story and to the difficulties he was having in the writing: "I have determined to write it all over when I have time, which accounts for your not having it inflicted on you up to date. This course seemed to me best as soon as I heard from Mr. Scribner, though I had promised to let it be seen by others, and though Mr. S. made a suggestion relative to bringing it out in book form" (PC, May 25, 1887). However, his efforts to keep as many northern editors interested in it as possible were not successful, since he was himself unable for ten years to make the book anything better than "a political tract."

Page's is the extreme case of the unregenerate rebel who was yet able to place his stories in magazines largely unsympathetic to his point of view. While his work was fresh and new, he achieved remarkable successes; but, even with the assistance he received from Gilder and his other editors, his work deteriorated as he lost the freshness of his earliest approaches to fiction and became entangled with a dogmatic and illiberal theory of politics and race in the South. Although he published in *Harper's* and other northern magazines as well as in *The Century,* much of the credit for his development as a writer belongs to Gilder, who taught him most of what he knew about form in the short story.

II *Joel Chandler Harris*

Joel Chandler Harris was as talented in the writing of fiction as any writer in the South; yet Harris presented Gilder and the other editors of *The Century* with as difficult an editing problem as Page. Like Page, Harris was more inclined to write episodes or sketches than stories; but, unlike Page, Harris suffered from an excessive modesty that on occasion threatened his artistic production. Gilder found that only diligent praise and the most cautious criticism could serve to make him produce work of value.

Harris began publishing his Uncle Remus stories in the Atlanta *Constitution* in 1878. Credit for bringing Uncle Remus to the attention of a nation-wide audience belongs to D. Appleton and Company, who published *Uncle Remus: His Songs and His Sayings* in 1880, creating an immediate demand for the works of Harris in the North. Gilder was not slow in recognizing Harris's talents and in bidding for his writing. In a letter dated March 10, 1881, he wrote Harris of how interested the magazine was in his work; and he requested a chance to see anything that Harris did in the near future. "You are so much of an artist," he wrote, "that we do not like to suggest anything as to the *form* of the short story supposed," but requested only that Harris let *Scribner's Monthly* see the work.[4] His request was successful: a poem, "A Song of the Mole," appeared in *Scribner's Monthly's* regular light verse column, "Bric-a-Brac," in April, 1881; and a series of three Uncle Remus tales, under the general heading of "A Rainy Day with Uncle Remus," was published during June, July, and August, 1881.

Additional contributions were prevented by Harris's diffidence for nearly a whole year. On December 19, 1881, Harris sent the manuscript of an article entitled "The Mocking-Bird" to Gilder's associate editor, Robert Underwood Johnson. Johnson, unaware of Harris's lack of faith in his own work, returned the article for alterations in January, 1882, commenting: "We like the 'Mocking-Bird,' and in your humility of soul you must remember that it is accepted in good faith. Send it back when you can. If by any chance you should drop below your best standard—why, what are editors for? We shall certainly be frank with you;—frank in appreciation and in criticism." [5] But Harris, too modest to be satisfied with Johnson's reassurances about the value of the article, decided not to publish it. Replying to Johnson on January 25, 1882, Harris attempted to sketch the reasons for his lack of self-confidence. "Uncle Remus was a lucky accident," he wrote, "and perhaps I can do nothing else as well." Ignoring his achievements, he questioned his capacity to improve: "how *can* I reach the sublime heights of perfect simplicity as to style and method; Is a man too old to learn at thirty-two?" (HP).

Having lost "The Mocking-Bird," Gilder was careful not to return Harris's next contribution for even minor alterations. Four of Harris's "Plantation Ballads" appeared in *The Century* in May, 1882, and in January, 1883. Gilder had doubts about the advisability of printing them in "Bric-a-Brac," the magazine's only vehicle for light verse; but, rather than take the chance of losing them entirely by returning them to Harris for revision, he determined to print them in "Bric-a-Brac" after all (HP, Apr. 18, 1882).

In June, 1882, Harris made a short trip to New York, where for the first time Gilder and Johnson had an opportunity to observe his shyness. Harris confounded both of them by contracting stage fright a few hours before a dinner engagement and departing hastily for Atlanta (*LJCH*, 190). From that point on Gilder recognized the extent of his problem with Harris and measured his critical statements carefully to be kind to his timid genius.

Sometime late in 1882 Harris sent his first long story to Gilder, "At Teague Poteet's, A Story of the Hog Mountain Range," with a typical letter: "Enclosed you will find a sort of whatshisname. I'm afraid it is too episodical to suit serial publication—but after all, life itself is a series of episodes. Perhaps something else is the matter. If you don't find it available, you can at least give me some helpful suggestions" (*LJCH*, p. 201).

Gilder, who was very enthusiastic about the story, proposed to Harris that it be advertised as a novelette; but Harris objected to any description of it that promised more than the story attempted. Gilder quite naturally did not contravene Harris's wishes in the matter, but his reply was one more attempt to bolster Harris's self-confidence:

> I am afraid that in your modesty you think I am not sincere in what I have said of the merits of the piece. Such modesty is so *rare* that I forgive you the imputation. . . . As I think over the story I find it has left a very definite impression and a very agreeable human feeling . . . the whole Poteet household is full of life, and the heroine is not sentimentalized nor lifted out of her plane. . . . The MS. is not a 'failure'; it is definitely accepted in its present shape, in the belief that you can easily strengthen it. (*LJCH*, 202)

Johnson handled the details of the "strengthening" of "At Teague Poteet's" with as much tact as Gilder had used in accepting it. Harris manifested his appreciation of the editors' work in several letters, one of which vows improved future work in one sentence and utter lack of self-confidence in the next: "I am going to write you a story and I hope it will be better than 'Teague Poteet.' The great difficulty is that the great things that I map out in my mind are utterly dissipated by the process of composition." [6]

One element that must have caused the editors some uneasiness over the manuscript of "Teague Poteet" is scrupulously unmentioned in the correspondence with Harris about its publication. The story deals in some detail with an illegal distillery, and certain rather unsavory characters are presented quite sympathetically. Apparently, once the editorial decision had been made to accept the story, which is certainly a moral one in its total aspect, Gilder prepared to defend it against critics who might find its subject matter unwholesome. Nothing was said to Harris about this side of the story, but Gilder referred to it obliquely in his speech on southern literature in which he stated that southern authors could be "sympathetic with the . . . illicit distiller . . . with the sinner though not with the sin." Clearly, he was refer-

ring to "At Teague Poteet's," in which such a division of sympathy
is an important issue.

Immediately following "At Teague Poteet's" in *The Century*
were three more Uncle Remus stories under the general heading
of "Nights with Uncle Remus." At about this time Century Company offered Harris a contract to write exclusively for it. Such an
arrangement would have freed him from the newspaper hack-
work he was forced to do for the Atlanta *Constitution;* but Harris,
too doubtful of his ability to produce good fiction consistently,
refused the offer(*LJCH*, 214).

His refusal to work under contract to *The Century* did not stop
the flow of stories, poems, and dialect sketches submitted to the
magazine. " 'Free Joe' and the Rest of the World," Harris's own
favorite among his stories, appeared in November, 1884. It was
followed by "Trouble on Lost Mountain," received in August,
1885, and not printed until January, 1886, chiefly because of the
crush of articles for *The Century's* "War Series," then at its height.
The story was a direct result of a short tour commissioned by Gilder for Harris and the illustrator assigned to his next few stories,
A. B. Frost. The resulting illustrations pleased Harris very much.
"Mr. Frost's illustrations," he wrote Robert Underwood Johnson,
"are so true to the spirit of the text that they seem to be an echo of
my own mind. . . . It has been so difficult, you know, to prevent
a northern artist from misrepresenting southern life and character." [7]

"Trouble on Lost Mountain" caused very little editorial difficulty. Gilder twice wrote Harris praising the story, and there was
apparently little or no revision necessary. That was not the case
with "Little Compton," Harris's next story. The manuscript as first
submitted to Gilder was unacceptable; but, rather than reject it,
Gilder returned it with a long list of possible improvements and
corrections. Harris made some of them, commenting that Gilder's
letter had "paralyzed" him. He returned the story in July, 1886,
with an accompanying letter that blamed the falling off of his
work partly on his newspaper work and partly on "fatty degeneration of the mind" (*LJCH*, 221). In Gilder's reply one month later,
he congratulated Harris on the improvements he had made in the
story, then tactfully objected: "But it is so full of dramatic situations that to have none at all at the end leaves the reader with a
sense of soreness." He suggested two other improvements, even to

the extent of writing several paragraphs of dialogue; and he ended the letter with more words of praise for the story in general (HP, Aug. 21, 1886). Harris adopted Gilder's suggestions, word for word in some cases; and the story was printed to a good deal of acclaim in April, 1887.

The history of the publication of Harris's next important story for *The Century*, "Azalia," was complicated by two disagreements between the author and the editor on matters that are quite significant in terms of Gilder's editorial criticism. Gilder accepted the story in a letter of December 14, 1886, saying that it was the "best first draft of a story you have sent here except 'Trouble on Lost Mountain.' It has not the complete dramatic unity of that story, but it is much better in that respect than the first draft of 'Little Compton'" (HP). The most important defect Gilder found in the construction of the story was Harris's treatment of a scene in which the heroine discovers that her brother, who she knew had died fighting for the North in the Civil War, had been respectfully buried by the southern family with whom she is staying in the story. "The reader," Gilder complained, "has already 'caught on' to this, and when he comes to it the point is made in rather a flat way."

Further on in the same letter Gilder generalized from his criticism, softening his censure of Harris's weak structure with praise for everything else: "I feel that this matter of dramatic construction is one that you ought to more closely consider, for in every respect your stories are—I was going to say beyond criticism. They are vital, humorous, pathetic, tragic, and full of character." In the same letter Gilder mentioned that he particularly enjoyed "the story of the footprint" in "Azalia," which he had, coincidently, heard only a few weeks before. This refers to an incident in the story in which a mother preserves under a trap-door-like arrangement the only souvenir she has of her recently deceased son—his footprint in the clay of the cabin's floor.

Harris replied with assurances that he was "willing to adopt any suggestions" Gilder might care to make that were aimed at improving the story. As for the footprint story, he included a complete provenance for the incident. He had, he wrote, obtained the story from a southern woman who vouched for its accuracy, adding, "however, I'm not afraid to use it, nor any other similar episode that may fall in my way. When human nature goes to inven-

tion, her inventions are the property of the first to use them"
(*LJCH*, 224). Gilder's answer to this letter seems not to have survived, but it must have angered Harris somehow. His next letter
was one of the angriest outbursts the mild-mannered creator of
Uncle Remus ever allowed himself. He began by taking Gilder to
task. "Come! Are you going to confine us all to invention of our
own? Are we, who are working in a comparatively new field, to
take no advantage of the legends, the traditions and the happenings with which we are familiar? . . . The Footprint business
. . . is beyond invention. It is real. It belongs to human nature.
It is mine if I re-create characters that would be apt to employ it."
He then ended the letter with an assurance that Gilder was free to
return the "vile affair," the manuscript, if he objected to the footprint incident (*LJCH*, 225–6).

Gilder quickly denied any intention to prohibit a writer from
using the "traditions, legends, and happenings" of the people
about whom he was writing. "You are entirely and colossally mistaken," he wrote, "in your supposition that I object to the use of
real events, real traits and situations in fiction. Let me disabuse
your mind entirely of any such supposition." What concerned Gilder, though he did not say it outright in his letter, was the difference between an author's and an editor's awareness of the laws of
libel and copyright. He had no objection to real events in fiction
so long as the author was a man of honor and aware of the difference between a plagiarism, a slander, and a usable anecdote. Harris, he was sure, was such a man, and his previous letter was in no
sense intended to suggest otherwise (HP, Dec. 29, 1886). One can
imagine the sighs of relief from both parties when this letter
closed the dispute.

But the difficulties with the story did not end there, for the
problem of the lack of dramatic construction remained. On March
12, 1887, Harris wrote that he had "added greatly to the story so
far as length is concerned, and have tried to meet your views in
shaping it." [8] Gilder wrote on April 20, 1887, his approval of Harris's additions as far as they had gone, but added: "You don't give
a man any satisfaction about that scene [i.e., where the heroine
discovers the whereabouts of her brother's body] in your new
story. To me the story will be 75% per cent [*sic*] less good than it
may be if you don't brace up that climacteric scene" (GP). Harris

worked over the scene but was entirely unsatisfied with the results. He next attempted to justify it as originally written:

> Consider the situation! Here is a young woman who has lost her only brother. Her grief for his death—she knows he is dead—is sincere, but the shock of it is past. Suddenly she discovers that the brother whom she mourns as both dead and lost, has received a decent burial in this out-of-the-way place. She is astonished, of course, but her astonishment gives no basis for a scene, for with her knowledge of the fact there must also be a feeling of gratification. Turn it as I may, this seems to be the inevitable conclusion. (*LJCH*, 227)

Gilder's reply is equivocal, apparently evincing satisfaction with what changes Harris had made and denying any intention of changing the scene to one of melodrama: "Now I see that you have turned your giant mind on the great point at issue—I am better pleased. But mind you, I did not mean that I wanted you to fire off a keg of gunpowder at the point mentioned. There seemed something lacking—I don't know what. Perhaps it was too intense instead of not intense enough, and perhaps, always, perhaps I was mistaken" (GP, Apr. 30 [1887]).

The scene as printed suggests that Harris's final summary of the situation and the emotions of the heroine convinced Gilder that no other revision was necessary. The printed version includes only a brief exclamation on the part of the heroine, followed with an aside by the author:

> It would be difficult, under all the circumstances, to describe Helen's thoughts. She was gratified—she was more than gratified—at the unexpected discovery, and she was grateful to those who had cared for her brother's grave with such scrupulous care. She felt more at home than ever. The last barrier of sectional reserve (if it may be so termed) was broken down so far as she was concerned, and during the remainder of her stay, her true character—her womanliness, her tenderness, her humor—revealed itself to these watchful and sensitive southerners. (XXXIV, 885–6)

Harris gave his post-publication opinion of the story in a letter to Charles Scribner: "I see that Mr. R. H. Stoddard says that 'Azalia' is 'exquisite and pathetic,' but if that affair isn't trash from the word go, then I don't know what trash is" (*LJCH*, 228-9). This statement in no way reflects anger or annoyance at Gilder's tinkering with his manuscript. Harris, perhaps more than any other writer who contributed to *The Century*, appreciated editorial help whenever he received it. Rather, his comment was a result of a suspicion that any story of his that required so much help and criticism from Gilder must have been "trash from the word go."

Harris continued as a more-or-less constant contributor to *The Century* through his lifetime, but his work declined through the 1890's. His real forte was the slice-of-life sketch in dialect, but unfortunately his inclinations moved in another direction—toward sentimentalism. By 1901 Gilder could write him on August 15 that *The Century* would be interested in his proposed long story, "The Death of Uncle Remus," as soon as he could finish it "with all the deliberation that you desire and which it really ought to have," but that the editors were more interested in a "little story or incident" in the meanwhile (HP). Clearly, by that time Gilder was despairing of the problem of bending Harris's sketches into a short-story format. Harris had despaired of the same problem, for he wrote in 1894 that he had forsworn all efforts to make his sketches conform to the then rather dogmatic principles about the form of the short story. "My whole aim," he wrote, "has been at *life* and *character*, and I have purposely left the *style* to take care of itself." [9] Style in an Uncle Remus story was almost entirely a function of dialect, of which Harris was a master; but in his later stories and novels of the poor whites of the South, his style was not subtle enough to carry through the rather intense effects he attempted. With deficiencies of that magnitude, Harris could be helped by no editor.

Gilder's aid to Harris was in three areas. First, he provided a magazine of large circulation, the largest in the country during the period of Harris's most frequent contributions, to give currency to Harris's best stories and characters. To Harris, who had done most of his short-story publishing in the South before *The Century* adopted him, such wide circulation was a great help to his always doubtful self-confidence. Second, Gilder used every psychological device at his command to boost Harris's confidence in his work, flattering twice for every criticism, and in some cases printing works of which the author was ashamed. Third, Gilder cajoled Harris into spending more effort on the style and form of his productions than he was wont to do, turning sketches into short stories, giving continuity to isolated incidents, adding dramatic interest to stories developed as flat narratives, and generally turning anecdotes into readable and artistic stories. In this, of course, he was not alone; but, of all Harris's editors, he was certainly the most influential and probably did more than anyone else to keep Harris's work at its highest artistic level.

III George Washington Cable

Of all the southern contributors to *Scribner's Monthly* and to *The Century*, none scored a greater success or became finally a greater disappointment than Cable. He was completely unknown when Edward King called Gilder's attention to his short stories.[10] His first accepted story, " 'Sieur George," excited Gilder. "He is a genius," Gilder wrote King, "and he ought to know it. If he's a man it won't hurt him" (GP, Aug. 29, 1873). To Cable himself, though, Gilder tempered his enthusiasm with some editorial advice. If he would strive for greater clarity and precision in his prose, Cable was assured by Gilder that he could become "one of the best story writers of the day." [11] The contrast between Gilder's statements to King and to Cable seems devious, but was appropriate under the circumstances. Cable needed some unalloyed praise after his years of unfruitful work. As Cable's editor, Gilder needed to be free to criticize, while King was in a position to praise Cable without reservations. Gilder perhaps instinctively recognized that Cable would someday need a corrective editorial hand.

Although five more of Cable's stories were accepted by Gilder and printed in *Scribner's Monthly* between 1874 and 1876, their success was offset by Gilder's failure to accept one of Cable's best and most popular stories, " 'Posson' Jone.'" Gilder's reasons for rejecting the story are not hard to deduce. " 'Posson' Jone,'" unlike all Cable's other early stories, is broadly comic. Briefly stated, it tells how Jules St. Ange, a Creole picaro in the great tradition, attempts to relieve a West Florida preacher, Parson Jones, of some money belonging to the "Smyrny" church of which Jones is the innocently Christ-like pastor. Jules, who succeeds in getting Jones drunk, leads him to violate the sabbath in several most amusing and shocking ways. Jones engages in a wrestling bout with a tiger and a buffalo, and, inevitably, is thrown into jail. But the parson's manliness-cum-piety converts Jules, and in the end Jules is saved from a life of crime through his exposure to the man of God. The narrative moves in a confusing fashion, and there is too much plot in a short span; but the two characters, Jules and Jones, are among the liveliest ever invented by Cable.

When Gilder read it, he must have recognized that it was a new departure for Cable from the tighter woven, more delicate stories he had previously submitted. The structural flaws in the story alone might well have convinced him that this new departure was not all to the good. Also, Holland's influence upon the editorial policies of *Scribner's Monthly* was still relatively strong in 1875, and he probably objected to publishing a story in which a drunken minister fights animals in an arena. Whatever the reasons, the rejection of the story was later regretted by Gilder. It is worth noting, however, that other editors made the same mistake; " 'Posson' Jone" was refused by the *New York Times, Galaxy*, and *Harper's Monthly* before it was accepted by *Appleton's Journal* and published in April, 1876.

All six of the stories that appeared in *Scribner's Monthly* during Cable's first years as a writer were edited to some extent before publication. Some, like " 'Sieur George," were revised for structural reasons; others had what Gilder called "little awkwardnesses" removed. Along with his specific editorial advice and criticism of Cable's work, Gilder also embarked Cable on a literary self-improvement program. He recommended certain authors, from whom he thought Cable might profit, including Turgenev, " a master worth any artist's study." [12] Much of his editing and his advice was intended to strengthen Cable's writing; some of it was to make Cable's stories more acceptable to a "family magazine." Gilder's exact purposes may never be known, but the opinion of one modern critic is probably a fair estimate: "Gilder's editing of Cable can be summed up as an attempt to adapt him to a widely circulated magazine without sacrificing his distinguishing excellence." [13] Stated less negatively, Gilder tried to bring Cable to the highest possibilities of his talent without jeopardizing the standing of *Scribner's Monthly* with its readers.

Gilder was in Europe when Cable's first novel, *The Grandissimes*, was being serialized in *Scribner's Monthly*; thus he had nothing to do with the editing of Cable's finest work. He had a great deal to do with Cable's second novel, however. In 1881 Cable began work on *Dr. Sevier* while he was engaged in a prison-reform movement in New Orleans. The first draft of the novel, which he had tentatively entitled "Bread," he sent off to Gilder in January, 1882. Gilder replied with a long letter that has great bearing on their relationship and upon Gilder's editorial method. The letter begins with a wish that the Fates had not placed Gilder in a position where he must judge his "betters," and it ends with an apology for his "brutal attack," which he feels is justified because his "whole heart" is involved in Cable's success and he "cannot keep from plain speech." In between is some of Gilder's best editorial advice and some of his finest criticism, especially on the uses of the didactic:

Now, about "Bread." To me it is the least good work you have ever done. And yet it has in it some of your best work, and it is free from your greatest fault, namely confusion.

I will not condemn myself by suspecting that you imagine that I object to the inculcation of morality, religion, or any kind of spiritual truth in a work of art. I will not condemn you by letting you suspect that I doubt your theories on this subject. I am sure that we both agree that it may be done, and that the question only is, is it well done! It seems to me that in the present story (if it is a story) your heart has got the better of your head. The story to me fails of its end because the motive is too apparent. The reader feels that it is a "put up job"; that the characters are dragged from misery to misery in order that the writer can preach his theories through them. The Dr. the clerk and the nurse are the only real figures in the book. The two principal characters are lay figures, "objects" of sympathy. You have turned your mind lately so completely into philanthropical work that for the time being you have lost your sense of art. I do not object to the philanthropy either in life . . . [or] in this book—but its expression must—in a work of art—take an artistic form. You and I do not object to the morality and spiritual teaching of Hawthorne, and to the patriotism and philanthropy of Tourguenieff . . . because the form is always artistic.

My dear fellow, I care more for your work than for any other writer of fiction who has written for the magazine. As an editor I should not, perhaps, say this; as a friend I cannot help it. Now there are many things that spoil a literary career, sometimes a lack of conscience, . . . sometimes an untrained or misapplied conscience. . . . For heaven's sake do not lose, break, or injure the vehicle that you possess and that, under your direction, carries spiritual food, no less than intellectual stimulus and wholesome pleasure to so many minds.[14]

This letter, no doubt very painful for Gilder to write, was followed by several others which continued to be apologetic about the necessity for criticism, while assuming both the right and the need to criticize. On the next day Gilder softened some of the criticism of the first letter with praise for certain situations and characters in the novel. But Gilder stressed again the necessity to make the novel "less obviously a story of intention." He understood Cable's need for pointedness, but he insisted once more on an artful exposition: "I doubt if you can . . . fully conceal the philanthropic bent. It is a glorious bent, in itself, if the writer does not betray himself" (GL, Feb. 2, 1882).

Upon receiving Cable's acknowledgement of his first letter, Gilder wrote again about the possibilities of the novel. Cable could surely "make a good book out of most of those characters . . . and the opening vista of the war is just stunning." Two months later he received the revisions of the first few chapters and telegraphed Cable his congratulations, following the telegram with a letter of more specific encouragement. "If you keep on at that rate," he wrote, "you will have a fortunate journey and a capital book. Such fine artistic work warms the cockles of an editor's heart" (LRWG, 391). In all, Cable wrote three drafts of the novel, and it was not until June, 1883, that Gilder accepted it. *Dr. Sevier* ran in *The Century* from November, 1883, to October, 1884. It was well received, but did not get the extravagant praise given *The Grandissimes*.

While *Dr. Sevier* was being serialized, Cable turned his attention more specifically to the plight of the Negro in the South than he had yet done with his fiction; and again Gilder supported him. "The Freedman's Case in Equity," Cable's first specific attack upon the South's treatment of the Negro minority, was published in *The Century* in January, 1884. It was probably the most controversial article ever published by Gilder, and it brought upon the magazine and its editor a storm of abuse. Gilder responded by defending Cable against his antagonists—both by mail and personally. He attended the New Orleans exposition of 1884 to give his moral and vocal support to Cable during a period when all Cable's neighbors had become his critics.[15] He refused to print letters abusing Cable and the article in the magazine. To writers of such letters he replied in a form letter, "If the South wishes to defame and persecute its brightest literary ornament and leading writer, it is welcome to do so, but the persecution cannot be carried on within our columns" (GP, July 15, 1885). Instead, Gilder invited Henry W. Grady, editor of the Atlanta *Constitution* to reply. Grady's article, "In Plain Black and White," was then followed by a rebuttal by Cable, "The Silent South."

Gilder's sympathy with Cable's point of view was based on a liberal concept of the southern problem. Critics who have found his editorial policy to be one of acceptance of southern racial separation have not considered his courage in printing these articles by Cable. Gilder stated his position frankly enough in a letter to Grady concerning his article (GP, May 15, 1885). Argument based on fear of "miscegenation is a humbug and a fraud," he wrote. Such emotional appeals can only delay the day when "the color line would disappear from your laws." To Gilder, the social evolution of the Negro in the South was inevitable and attempts at delay were not only senseless but positively harmful since they increased the friction between races. "Can there be any true peace with any other solution?" he asked Grady. Though he tolerated certain southern fiction based on a segregationist ethic, Gilder could throw all his efforts into support of Cable's position when the controversy was specifically about Negro rights.

Editors do not *enjoy* printing unprofitable and controversial articles in the pages of their magazines, and Gilder was no exception. Sympathetic as he was to Cable's views, he restricted the discussion to three articles. When Cable made an effort to revive the question some years later by recommending an inflammatory article by his friend Charles Waddell Chesnutt, Gilder strategically demurred: "Mr. Chesnutt's paper—'The Negro's Answer to the Negro Question,' is a timely political paper. So timely and *so* political—in fact so partisan—that we cannot handle it. It should appear at once somewhere." [16] Sympathetic as he was, Gilder found it necessary to deny his sympathy to what was obviously a lost and unprofitable cause.

Between 1885 and 1890 Gilder published most of Cable's work, but his writings of those years were more historical than literary.

They were followed by *John March, Southerner,* a novel that was
the first significant work of Cable's refused by Gilder since "'Posson' Jone." Cable wrote Gilder from Northampton, Massachusetts,
asking him to listen to a reading of the first two installments of the
novel. Cable, who was diffident about the novel, noted that it was
one which "after all you may not want to print, although I am
trying to put my very best into it" (GP, July 16, 1890). Gilder
replied with rather a prophetic impersonality that he was "scud-
ding under bare poles" that summer, and that it would be better
to "read the ms. without the personal element" (GP, July 17,
1890). His tone suggests that Gilder feared the manuscript would
disappoint him. Cable hired a secretary to make a fair copy of the
finished part of the novel and sent it to Gilder in August, 1890.
When Gilder read it, he is said to have wrung his hands in de-
spair. He wrote Cable that he could "weep for disappointment,"
that, like the first draft of *Dr. Sevier,* the new novel was more
tract than fiction, that it was, "instead of a return to literature, an
attempt to fetch everything into literature save and except literature itself. . . . Shades of [Albion] Tourgée!"

A month later Gilder reverted to the "personal element" he had
wished to escape earlier. Apologizing for the harshness of his criticism, he added, "I wrote in great disappointment myself, for I had
great hopes for the book." [17] But his personal friendship with Cable
was not enough to persuade Gilder to accept the manuscript when
it was presented a second time in May, 1891, or even the third and
final time in June, 1893. These three rejections ended the close
editorial relationship between Cable and Gilder. Cable placed the
novel with *Scribner's Magazine,* in which it was serialized in 1894,
without attracting much interest; and he never again attempted to
publish his fiction (what little he produced) in *The Century.*

Though their editorial relationship was over, Gilder and Cable
remained friends. Cable often called on Gilder for help for
his "Home Culture" Clubs, wrote a biographical sketch of Gilder
for a series on "Editors of Great Magazines," and included Gilder
among the very close friends to whom he announced his second
marriage. During these last years Cable referred to Gilder as his
"old friend" whom he "loved dearly" (GP, Nov. 1, 1906). When
Gilder died, Cable testified in *The Century* that Gilder "was a
shaping, guiding influence, noble, invaluable, and endearing" to
himself and to "a multitude of other" writers (LXXIX, 634–5).

Gilder's most significant contribution to Cable's development as a writer was certainly the respect, admiration, and, withal, critical objectivity with which he viewed his work. To Cable, as to any young writer, such assistance is invaluable. Of that there can be no doubt; but Gilder had a shaping hand in Cable's development as a writer in two areas—his style and his trend toward didacticism—in which a judgment of Gilder's influence is much more important. Cable's writing, especially his early productions, exhibits a joy in language and style (at the expense of the reader's comprehension, it must be admitted) that is unlike the work of any writer of his period and reminds the modern reader of some of the works of Faulkner. To Gilder, whose experience proved to him that nothing was more desirable in a short story than clarity, Cable's peculiar style seemed charming, but also dangerous and in need of control. Gilder must have wondered often if Cable's confusion in syntax was stylistically effective—a means of involving the reader more deeply in the narrative—or if his writing was simply amateurish. Possibly Gilder did somewhat limit Cable's experimentation towards artful obscurantism, but he was the first editor to recognize that Cable's style was artistic. Unquestionably, much of Cable's early writing *is* amateurish; and it is even possible that Gilder helped Cable to understand the relationship between his style and the success of his writing.

Gilder's influence on Cable toward a more artistic expression of didactic purpose was a losing battle. Cable's writing suffered whenever he took on a "philanthropic bent," but all of his respect for Gilder's judgment on this one point could not save him from continuing steadily towards more obtrusive moral judgment in his work. Gilder's aversion to stories of purpose in which the moral or ideological objective is more evident than the story was nearly pathological, but it was also certainly critically sound. That he failed to convince Cable of the validity of this one premise was not his fault; Cable became more and more adamant concerning didacticism late in his life. Still, Gilder was Cable's most respected critic; and his failure to convince Cable that he must not "drag" his characters "from misery to misery," to "preach his theories through them," led as inevitably to Cable's final failure as a writer as to his break with Gilder as an editor. Judging from all the evidence, I do not think it can be argued that Gilder's failure resulted from lack of trying.

CHAPTER *4*

Turn East . . .

D OES the time make the man, or does the man make the time?
Gilder happened to arrive at a position of literary influence
at a time when American writers were crying for their independence, economic and esthetic, from the traditions of England. By
1880, the cry had been audible in America for more than half a
century, it is true; but it was during the twenty years of Gilder's
greatest power that the longest steps toward the realization of
American literary independence were taken. In 1891 an international copyright treaty was written, for the first time giving American writers status equal to that of English writers in competition
for American publishers. In 1885 the first masterpiece written in
the American idiom, *Huckleberry Finn,* may be said to have established the literary possibilities of the American language and
experience. Gilder helped to make both these events possible.

One of Gilder's firmest editorial policies was that of "America
first." His magazine actively cultivated an Americanism "that
deems the best of the Old World not too good for the New," as he
put it in one editorial (XLI, 148). And yet, it was Gilder too,
more than any other editor of the magazine, who was responsible
for the success of the English edition of the magazine—a considerable success that, in less than twenty years, made it more popular than any comparable British journal. Gilder's policy in regard
to the two points of this paradox was that of assiduously having
his cake and eating it too: of capturing a large circulation in England while keeping the magazine not only American in essence,
but, on many points positively antagonistic to British taste.

This apparently neat trick was not nearly so difficult as it
sounds. National bias had little effect upon the success of the
magazine in England. American magazines had simply developed
farther than English magazines in terms of typographic excellence, quality of illustrations, and editorial willingness to pay well-

known authors generous sums for their work. And, of all American magazines, *The Century* under Gilder was first and best in these qualities.[1] With this excellence to rely upon, Gilder could afford to publish, for example, Howells' article on Henry James, in which the "confidential attitude" of Thackeray and the "mannerism" of Dickens were criticized. He could weather the storm of English abuse which followed with comfortable certainty.

Still, we ought not to forget that Gilder *chose* to "turn West," when most other American magazines, especially those in New York, were still looking to England for many of their contributions. It is too easy to say that the time was right for Gilder's action and leave it at that. The truth is that Gilder's Americanism cost the magazine contributions and subscriptions, those tokens of popularity that no editor can dismiss lightly. Perhaps, even more important, Gilder's decision cost him at least one friendship which he valued very highly, that of Edmund Gosse. The tragi-comic story of the relationship of these two men illustrates, better than any other evidence, the full implications of this aspect of Gilder's editorial policy.

I *Gilder's Englishman*

It was through Gosse that Gilder made his first contacts with the English literary world. When the Gilders went to Europe for the first time in 1879, Gosse invited them several times to his home to meet, among others, Swinburne, Austin Dobson, and Robert Browning (GP, Dec. 29, 1879). Gosse's hospitality did not go unrewarded; Gilder suggested while he was still in Europe that Gosse be hired as English agent for the magazine (*LRWG*, 97). Holland rejected the idea in 1880; but, when Gilder took over the editorship of *The Century*, one of his first acts was to install Gosse as English representative (GL, June 16, 1881).

The history of Gosse's relationship with Gilder and Century Company after he became the company's English agent is a series of misapprehensions on both sides: on Gosse's, concerning the relative importance of the English edition of the magazine and the magazine's function; on Gilder's, about the esthetic tolerance of Gosse. Gosse's first duty as English agent was to entertain Roswell Smith on Smith's visit to London in June, 1881. Smith, a very religious man, travelled with his personal chaplain, a foible which made Gosse somewhat uneasy. "How very odd of Mr. R[oswell] S[mith] to travel with his parson!" he wrote Gilder. "I hope he is not tainted with teetotalism. Must one ask the parson too, if one persuades Mr. R.S. to come and see one?" (GP, June 13, 1881). Here was lesson number one for Gosse about the Anglo-American literary alliance to which he had just become a part.

Lesson number two followed shortly after. A letter from Gilder, mailed before he received the comments above, took Gosse to task for the propensity of English writers to lard their articles with foreign words and phrases. "We would like to avoid even the appearance of pedantry in the magazine," Gilder cautioned; "and we therefore beg you to warn writers against foreign languages." Without specifically making an invidious comparison between English and American magazines, Gilder made it clear that he believed "certain too scholarly phrases" might be all right for English journals, but that *The Century's* audience was too vast for them. "I think this is not an ignoble concession," he added, as if to rub salt in the wounds. "Every man can have an intellect as well as a soul and not be familiar with foreign languages" (GP, June 16, 1881).

Additional lessons for Gosse in the ways of America and *The Century Magazine* followed. Gilder found it necessary to point out several times to Gosse that *The Century* was not just a literary magazine, that all kinds of reform movements, from international copyright to urban renewal projects were supported by the magazine. One of his letters to Gosse is an urgent and earnest defense of the use of the magazine's pages for Civil Service reform, which to Gilder transcended national interest, but which must have seemed to Gosse evidence of Gilder's provincialism (GP, July 7, 1881). Another point of contention was in the area of theological and philosophical liberalism. When Gilder asked Gosse to have one English writer "modify his private confession of faith" in an article submitted to the magazine, he defended his editorial position on philosophical liberalism:

> It is true that we allow a wide latitude of opinion—among our writers are Jews, Catholics, Christians, and Nothings. It is true that we do not draw a very sharp line; but the line has to be drawn somewhere, and the editors reserve the right to draw it. We

think it no more than honest that a magazine whose principal audience (and an audience that mostly pays in advance, on trust) is of a certain opinion should not too rudely shock that opinion. We constantly go beyond our main audience in the direction of liberality of thought, but generally exercise something of the same reticence of individual opinion that all writers of, say, fiction exercise—Dickens, Thackeray, and, an instance more to the point, George Eliot—in writing for a popular audience. (GP, Dec. 21, 1881)

After these earliest misapprehensions had been cleared away, Gosse's career with Century Company moved smoothly for three years, until the start of the "War Series" in the magazine—the articles later collected as *Battles and Leaders of the Civil War.* When it first became apparent that the series would be a lengthy one, Gosse complained to Gilder that the publication of such an unesthetic series would surely lose subscribers in England. Gilder's reply was anything but conciliatory:

Is there nothing interesting to you but art and literature? Now let me tell you—I would rather have an article by Grant on a battle won by him, I would rather read it, print it, publish it, than twenty articles by Daudet on Mistral. And yet I knew all the Provençals— one of my happiest periods was the few days spent among them. . . . Provence, Anjou, they are among the magic words for me. But heavens, a great world-changing heroic event told by the hero of it! . . . All wars are, alas, bloody, and there is no blood in my sonnet, and in Dobson's song that you like. But is there nothing stirring in blood—in heroism, in devotion to a political and moral conviction. Yes, you ought to be proud of a magazine that is conducting to unparalleled success the longest enterprise yet undertaken by a periodical. Don't let literature and art make dilettantes of us! (GL, July 1, 1885)

Gosse replied that the series was not only dull to English readers but symptomatic of *The Century's* preoccupation with things American. Gilder, however, was unwilling to concede anything to the English taste about the series except to promise vaguely that he would try to get "a good deal about England" into it (GL, July 30, 1885). Alas for Gosse, the series continued until October,

1886; the articles included much less than a "good deal about England"; and it was followed immediately by the serialization of Nicolay and Hay's long *Life of Lincoln.*

Gilder tried to coat the pill of the new series for Gosse with an assurance that the "*Life of Lincoln* was of such significance to the world that the readers of England would be as taken with it as American readers." His own distrust of the English reception of the series led him, however, to contradict this statement in the very same letter when he noted that the project would not be advertised all at once because he was afraid a specific announcement would not "take in England, as there will be a great deal of it" (GP, Nov. 2, 1885). Since the *Life of Lincoln* was a great failure for the magazine generally, it was certainly at least as unsuccessful in England. Concern for the English reader, however, was not a factor either in the choice of the series or in its editing for publication.

The breaking point with Gosse on the matter of the importance of the English edition of the magazine came the following year. Apparently, Gosse was smoldering for some time under Gilder's neglect of the interests of the English readers of the magazine. Finally he devised a plan through which the imbalance could be overcome. He suggested that Gilder establish an "open letter" series from English contributors for which he and T. Fisher Unwin, *The Century's* publisher in England, would be responsible (GP, Oct. 14, 1886). Gilder replied that, while he was mildly interested in articles on foreign subjects, "the conviction is growing daily upon us that we must give place to our American writers." He then continued with a declaration of literary independence that is the more significant for the fact that, for the first time in American literary history, it came from a man in a position to support it:

> Our writers are being crushed by the lack of international copyright; few of them have a proper income, and it seems to us as if it must be our duty to think first of them. . . . Our safes are full of admirable short stories and serials which we scarcely have room for. If we should take any English serial today[,] it would crowd out some American story which, in our way of thinking, has greater claims upon us. Americans are interested in English and foreign subjects; but we prefer as a rule to have these articles written, or else to have the illustrations made, by Americans. This is not provincialism; it is simply a matter of obvious duty. Why should

American magazines let American authors starve while they go seeking after strange gods? The American policy has always been the policy of The Century but we feel more and more inclined to insist upon it. . . . When will we have a strong literature in this country if we do not give place to it? (GP [c. Feb., 1887])

Even after this outspoken statement from Gilder, Gosse apparently did not quite believe that any editor could prefer the works of Cable or Bret Harte to those of Andrew Lang, Stevenson, or Browning. To a second letter expressing this disbelief, Gilder replied at even greater length, restating many of the points of his earlier letter and discussing the philosophy behind *The Century's* policy. He concluded with a definite refusal to open any more of the magazine's columns than were then allotted to English authors. He hoped his letter would not seem "narrow, boycotting, or provincial"; but he added that "genuine provincialism" is more likely to be "the neglect of whatever may be admirable in the provinces for something which may be no better in the metropolis" (GP, Mar. 7, 1887). Thoroughly chastened and convinced of Gilder's complete seriousness in the matter, Gosse replied in his next letter that he considered the matter closed, apologized for his part in it, and signed his letter "penitent Peter." [2]

Two years later Gosse announced that he would accept a position similar to the one he had with Century Company for S. S. McClure's "Associated Literary Press," a literary syndicate of the type then cutting into the circulation of magazines like *The Century.* He assured Gilder that such a division of his interests would "interfere in no degree with such now attenuated help as it is my privilege to render the 'Century Co'" (GP, Apr. 16, 1889). Both his tone and his language suggest that there was not a little bitterness in his feelings about Gilder's treatment of both the English edition and the company's English agent. The honeymoon was over, and the bride left with another man.

Gosse was not the only English writer connected with *The Century Magazine,* but his connection lasted the longest. In an editorial explaining the success of American periodicals in England, Gilder called attention to one of the reasons "for the willingness of some of the ablest of English writers to publish originally in American periodicals." Although America "has not produced as many first-class authors contemporaneously as has Great Britain, nevertheless America, with her fifty millions of people, is the country of readers, and too, of intelligent readers" (XXII, 146). He might have added two more reasons: American magazines were willing to pay more money for contributions than were English magazines, and there were not enough good American writers to keep the pages of magazines like *Scribner's Monthly* filled. In the case of *Scribner's Monthly* and *The Century*, that last consideration was the most important one. When the editorial files became filled with American contributions, English contributors were no longer so welcome as they had been.

Although Gilder balked at Gosse's suggestion of a regular department of contributions from English sources, he was eager for contributions of better than average quality from any source. That is, contributions were welcome; but *commitments* to accept contributions were unwelcome, at least from English sources. It should always be remembered that Gilder's Americanism evolved with the magazine and could not become firmly entrenched to the exclusion of non-American contributions until the supply of American writings became adequate both in quantity and quality. That situation, it need hardly be stated, was not really to come about until long after Gilder's death. Thus English contributions were never entirely absent from the magazine, although they were present in continually decreasing numbers during Gilder's editorship.

Under Holland, the magazine was almost more English than American. The first serial novel published in *Scribner's Monthly* was written by George MacDonald; Mrs. Oliphant, Mrs. Ward, and Mrs. West also contributed fiction to the magazine under Holland's urging. During Gilder's nearly thirty years as editor-in-chief of *The Century* such English writers as Walter Besant, William Watson, Austin Dobson, Andrew Lang, James Anthony Froude, William Morris, Christina Rossetti, Rudyard Kipling, and Robert Louis Stevenson, among many others, appeared in the magazine. Indeed, a complete list of the English contributors would make one wonder why the magazine should be considered typically American. But, of course, they represent only a small percentage —and a percentage in constant diminution—of the total number of contributors during Gilder's editorship.

Furthermore, there is often something subtly "American" about the flavor of many of the English contributions to *Century*. Kipling's contributions to the magazine, a serialized novel *The Nau-lahka* (written in collaboration with Wolcott Balestier) and the short story "The Brushwood Boy," were written by an American-ized Kipling, living in Brattleboro, Vermont. Stevenson's series of sketches on California gold-mining local color, *The Silverado Squatters*, was eagerly solicited by Gilder, eagerly accepted. But a second series suggested by Stevenson, based on a tour of the Rhone River, never materialized, in spite of Gilder's profound de-sire to help a friend in economic and physical difficulties (*LRWG* 120–1). Perhaps the best evidence of all concerning Gil-der's feelings about the relative merits of turning East or turning West may be found in the story of his relationship with that writer who struggled hardest with the same problem in regard to his own sources and traditions.

II *Henry James*

Henry James was the first really important writer cultivated by *Scribner's Monthly*. Holland recognized the talent exhibited in his earliest stories published in *The Atlantic* and *Galaxy*, and he pre-sumed on his friendship with Henry James, Sr., to intercede with his son for a contribution to *Scribner's Monthly*. In spite of the opposition of Howells, who was then feuding with Holland from his position as editor of *The Atlantic*, James contributed five sto-ries to Holland's magazine between 1874 and 1878. When Gilder became editor of *The Century*, he recultivated James, who had contributed nothing to the magazine for three years. He had James write an article on Venice early in 1882 and urged him to write more. A few months later, James submitted a story and a dramatized version of *Daisy Miller*. Gilder was pleased with the story, but he was not so certain about the play. His indecision was reflected in a letter to Roswell Smith, the business manager of the magazine:

> Mr. James has sent us a story which is so long it must be printed in two parts, called "The Point of View." It is accepted and Mr. Johnson says it is one of his best things. He wants [$]600 for it— & we will pay that. He is doing capital work for us by the way— the article on Venice and so forth.
> But he wants $1500 . . . for his dramatic version of Daisy

Miller—which would go into three parts, entirely rewritten—with a new denouement! It is, say, 38 pages long, and the "eds" do not feel warranted in paying the price. . . . No one has read it but me. It is very bright and interesting, and the plot seems to be new, but it is not so simple & charming & intense in its interest as the original story. . . . I think it would be an experiment worth trying [but] the opinion in the office is that it would be risky to pay more than $20 a page for it. I beg leave to leave the matter in your hands. (GL, Aug. 1, 1882)

This letter—really an "inter-office memo"—is unusual in several aspects. It is the only instance in which an editorial decision is referred to the business office of the magazine—the only instance in the records of more than thirty years of editing! It is a letter reflecting not merely a division of opinion in the editorial office, but a division in the mind of the editor-in-chief himself. Gilder suffered from ambivalent feelings about James throughout their long association. He was aware of James's genius from the first; but, unhappily, he was equally aware that James's extraordinary style could never appeal to a very large audience. He was therefore willing to extol James as a writer, to publish appreciative articles about his writing, and to accept his non-fiction gladly. But he was hesitant about James's fiction and positively frightened at the prospect of dealing with a play by James—the drama being that hobby-horse which most critics would agree James rode very badly. Nevertheless, James was a prestigious American writer and a personal friend. His contributions were welcome to Gilder, even though many of them caused him some very troublesome reflections.

When James submitted the first few chapters of *The Bostonians* to *The Century*, Gilder must have felt that here at last was an opportunity to do James justice in the magazine without jeopardizing the subscription lists. His letter accepting the novel for serialization bubbles with optimism and praise for what he had read: "I have just been reading two parts . . . of The Bostonians, and I cannot refrain from telling you how keenly I have enjoyed it. It is so *human*, with all the penetration, and humor of situation developed so charmingly. The style is so alert, the tone is a delight and refreshment" (GL, Nov. 14, 1884).

Within a few months Gilder was forced to change his mind about the novel. Long before its run in the magazine was over, it became a legend in *The Century* offices as the epitome of dullness. One of the editors recounted a typical anecdote. When, in the fall of 1885, Robert Underwood Johnson was making out the schedule for the following six months, he called out, " 'Carey! Oh, Carey, does "The Bostonians" end in February?' 'Yes,' replied Carey, not looking up from his own work. 'James says it does, and so does Tooker [another editor of the magazine], and they ought to know; they are the only ones who have ever read it.' " [3]

A third reader was Gilder, but he too was depressed by the lack of interest in the novel on the part of *The Century's* readers. After four installments had appeared, Gilder was so distressed by the novel's slow pace that he wrote an utterly untypical letter to James criticizing it, in the hope that James might tighten up the action in the remaining installments. The letter is one clear-cut example of an attempt by Gilder to influence a writer in a specific direction, an attempt which was entirely unsuccessful:

Leaving aside any question as to literary merit, I am afraid Mr. Howells has beaten you in the matter of readers.[4] The movement of "The Bostonians" is so slow that people seem to be dropping off from it. To me it is extremely enjoyable, but I can see reasons for impatience on the part of the readers. I notice that there is some repetition which you seem to acknowledge yourself by the expression "As I said before," or words to that effect. I never see anything that I could omit, supposing—what is ludicrously impossible—myself to be the author, but I sometimes wonder whether the art would not be better if something of Tourgenieff's condensation were used. I would not speak in this way were it not for a sense that a great many people were losing the pleasure of the story who would naturally like it, having made up their minds with the May number to the length to which it was being drawn out. If this feeling is so strong by the May number, I am afraid that when it comes to subsequent numbers it will be rather increased than diminished. Notwithstanding all this I am sure the book will be considered one of your very best, and as I said it is to me a constant source of interest.

P.S. My letter sounds, on reading it over, like a literary lecture! So much for the formality of punctuated words! Pray pardon any

apparent impertinence and believe me always your sincere friend
and admirer, R. W. Gilder. (GP, May 18, 1885)

Perhaps because of this letter, perhaps because of the change in
James's style which was taking place at just this period, few other
works by Henry James appeared in *The Century*. It is likely that
James submitted nothing more for some time because the reception of *The Bostonians* proved to him that *The Century's* audience
could not appreciate the subtle character of his work. There is no
question that the popular failure of the novel (and perhaps Gilder's rather patronizing letter pointing out that fact) nettled him.
Thirty years later he referred to the incident in a way that shows
it was still fresh in his mind. Answering some praises Edmund
Gosse had bestowed upon *The Bostonians*, James wrote:

> Your good impression of The Bostonians greatly moves me—the
> thing was no success whatever on publication in the Century
> (where it came out) and the late R. W. Gilder, of that periodical,
> wrote me at the time that they had never published anything
> that appeared so little to interest their readers. I felt about it then
> that it was probably rather a remarkable feat of objectivity—
> but I never was very thoroughly happy about it, and seem to re-
> call that I found the subject and the material, after I had got
> couched in it, under some illusion, less interesting and repaying
> than I had assumed it to be.[5]

That James thought *The Bostonians* at least a partial failure is
also suggested by the fact that it was not one of the novels he
revised for his collected works. Nonetheless, though he may have
agreed with Gilder's diagnosis of what was wrong with the novel,
he certainly did not take Gilder's advice—either then or thereafter
—that "something of Tourgenieff's condensation" might be valuable for his style.

To consider James's relationship with Gilder as a whole, we
must remove to the realm of hypothesis; documentary evidence
simply does not exist to explain why James's contributions to *The
Century* should have been so considerable before 1886 and so rare
thereafter. Gilder, to the end of his life, believed James to be, with
Twain and Howells, one of the three greatest living writers of
American fiction. It seems probable that James's exile from *The
Century* after 1886 was partially self-imposed, partially encour-

aged by Gilder, for two reasons. First, both James and Gilder realized after the fiasco of *The Bostonians* that *The Century,* with its
massive and essentially middle-class audience, was obviously not
the best vehicle for James's prose in America. The tendency evident in Gilder's requests for non-fiction from James before *The
Bostonians* appeared was buttressed by the failure of the novel,
and Gilder never requested anything but non-fiction from him
thereafter. James, on the other hand, preferred not to write non-
fiction after 1886. Instead, he explored more deeply the vein of
narrative objectivity which he had opened experimentally in *The
Bostonians.* Thus neither James nor Gilder, neither *The Century*
nor the fiction James wrote, moved toward accommodating each
other.

Second, Gilder very likely discriminated against James, consciously or unconsciously, because of a complex of feelings about
James's success as a writer and his voluntary expatriation from
America. James, by 1886, had become both a very successful
writer and English in his orientation. Gilder, an editor, who, in
Hamlin Garland's words, "looked for genius in every mail," was
far more interested in discovering new talent in an American than
in subsidizing developed (but unpopular) talent in a converted
Englishman. The combination of James's lack of popularity with
The Century's audience and his slighting of America combined in
Gilder's mind to make him a less desirable contributor than many
writers who had far less talent. Such must have been Gilder's reasons for neglecting a writer whom he knew and liked personally
and who was always regarded by Gilder as one of America's finest
writers. James turned East; Gilder, as we shall see, turned West.

CHAPTER *5*

... Turn West

THE rejection and gradual displacement of English writers
for *The Century* left a void which was only gradually filled
by western writers. As we have seen, Gilder's first regional preference was for the South. And, although he strongly objected to the
imputation, Gilder did "make a specialty," of southern literature,
at least to the extent that the pages of his magazine were limited
in their capacity to include regional fiction from other areas.
Through the 1870's and 1880's in particular, when the vogue of
southern local color was at its height, Gilder published a dispro-
portionate amount of southern fiction in his magazine. But the
apparent dependence of the magazine upon the South was somewhat illusory, for it was based almost entirely on supply and demand. From the publication of Edward King's "Great South"
series to the end of "Battles and Leaders of the Civil War," the
demand for southern fiction was at its highest, while the supply
was constant and of a fairly uniform quality. Gilder actually ex-
pended almost no effort to obtain southern fiction; the magazine's reputation was such that the manuscripts flowed to it
whether the editor wanted them or not. Even during the period
when southern contributions were at their peak in the magazine,
Gilder worked much harder to attract western contributors than
southern writers.

Gilder always felt a fascination for the vigorous new prose coming from the West. "How much I should like to see . . . a piece
of the great West," he wrote Roswell Smith, "the stalwart West—
The Blaine-loving, swaggering, hearty, enthusiastic, East-hating,
jealous West!" (GL, Aug. 20, 1884). Although *The Atlantic* led
The Century in the number and quality of western writings
published, Gilder succeeded in acquiring works by most of the
best western writers. In the eleven years of *Scribner's Monthly*
alone, Bret Harte and Joaquin Miller contributed one novel, ten

poems, and six short stories. Moreover, Gilder had to work much harder to get works by these men than writings by eastern or southern writers. To publish Miller's stories, Gilder entertained Miller at considerable expense when he came East in 1871. Bret Harte was pressed with an offer of more money than he was receiving from the *Overland Monthly* to become a regular contributor to *Scribner's Monthly*. Later, in order to keep him with the magazine, Roswell Smith actually became Harte's literary agent, promising to place any works for him which *Scribner's Monthly* could not use.[1]

These efforts to the contrary, Gilder was criticized for favoring contributions to *The Century* from the East and South over the West. In answer to one such criticism from Maurice Thompson, Gilder pointed out that he could never "accept articles from western . . . writers" only because they came from that area, but he could point out an honorable list of western writers in refutation: "Are Maurice Thompson, Mrs. Foote, Bill Nye, Hay and Nicolay, John Muir . . . Joaquin Miller, Edith Thomas, Edward Eggleston, Mark Twain . . . particularly eastern writers?" (GP, Nov. 1, 1886).

Gilder had reservations about the publication of western fiction in his magazine, but these limitations cannot be discovered by a quantitative analysis of western fiction in *The Century*. The peculiar difficulties he had as publisher of western writers are best seen in a rather intensive examination of his relationship with two writers who represent two schools, or perhaps better, *degrees* of local color emerging from the American Midwest and West: Edward Eggleston and Hamlin Garland. Conclusions drawn about these two men and the influence Gilder had on them may be extended to nearly all the western writers of Gilder's day.

I *Edward Eggleston*

It was Gilder who first turned Edward Eggleston to the writing of adult fiction. Just before the appearance of the first issue of *Scribner's Monthly*, Gilder sought out Eggleston, who had a small reputation as a writer of children's stories, and rather highhandedly announced, "Doctor, I will stop here on Monday morning next and get a story from you for our Thanksgiving number."[2] Eggleston later dedicated his first volume of short stories to Gilder, the man who "seduced" him into writing his first story. That story, "Huldah the Help," apparently did not arrive quite on "Monday morning," for it missed the November issue of the magazine and was printed in December, 1870. But its subtitle "A Thanksgiving Love-Story" clearly suggests the issue of the magazine it was intended for. The character and quality of all of Eggleston's early stories may be discovered from their titles and publication dates. Eggleston's second contribution bore the title "The Story of a Valentine" and appeared in the February, 1871, issue. His third story, "Ben: a Story for May-Day," came out in May, 1871. "The Gunpowder Plot," with a subtitle "The Story of a Fourth of July," was published in the July, 1871, issue.

Such "occasional" prose has as little literary value as we might expect. Yet the stories exhibit a constant improvement in the handling of the materials of local-color realism. In a very real sense Eggleston's early fiction and the magazine that printed it grew up at the same rate, and it is doubtful that "Huldah the Help" would have been accepted for publication in a magazine mature enough to print "The Gunpowder Plot." It is probably a fair statement (if an overburdening of the metaphor) that the first rather amateurish six months of *Scribner's Monthly* provided a nursery for Eggleston's fiction that was necessary for it to achieve full bloom.

At any rate, Eggleston's fourth contribution, "The Gunpowder Plot," exhibits all the characteristics of his mature work—both the stylistic flaws and the deftness of local-color technique. The plot, a wild tale of the Wisconsin frontier, is contrived, sentimental, and burdened with far too many coincidences. Eggleston's attempts to achieve verisimilitude vary from the most contrived afterthoughts to technically adept usage of first-person narration. This story marked something of a turning point in Eggleston's career: it is the first of his stories which exhibits an extensive use of local color for effect, and the first in which love interest is kept subordinate to a development of the interplay of character and locale. It was also a turning point in the character of his writing in another sense. His next contribution to *Scribner's Monthly* was entitled "Priscilla," but, though the story appeared in a November issue, the heroine was not the beloved of Myles Standish and John Alden, nor was there anything at all seasonal about it. Far from being overridden with plot like Eggleston's earlier stories, this one for the first time used the customs and standards of an Ohio town as

motivating forces for virtually all the action. Eggleston had succeeded in his search for the subject and method of his future writings.

Unfortunately for Gilder and *Scribner's Monthly,* just as Eggleston's mastery of the craft of fiction increased, so did his commitments to other magazines. During his first year of writing fiction,
Eggleston was an editor for *The Independent,* a curious publication, half-newspaper, half-magazine, which required no writing of
its editors. Then, in August, 1871, he left *The Independent* for
Hearth and Home, a more nearly literary magazine. He continued
to place occasional pieces in *Scribner's Monthly;* but, until he left
Hearth and Home in 1873, his fiction was needed for his own
magazine. Four of Eggleston's five first novels were serialized
there, including his most famous work, *The Hoosier Schoolmaster.*

Roxy was his first novel serialized in *Scribner's Monthly,* and his
first to be critically examined by an editor other than himself for
serial publication. He sent it to Gilder in the spring of 1877, and it
was accepted with only minor revisions. The events leading up to
the publication of his last novel, *The Faith Doctor,* tell a different
story, however, and suggest the extent of Gilder's influence upon
Eggleston. Eggleston worked on the novel during the spring and
summer of 1890; by the beginning of July, he was able to see the
end of it; and he wrote Gilder then that he would "give [him] a
chance to look at it as soon as possible" (GP, July 3, 1890). Gilder
was pleased with the manuscript when it arrived in August, but
he wrote Eggleston some criticisms, most of which were aimed at
eliminating the possibility of libel suits from real people mentioned in the novel. Eggleston's reply was prompt and polite, but
firm: Gilder's criticisms would have his "careful attention," he
wrote. "Anything which seems awry to you is to be suspected and
most critically examined, though of course the Century will give
me the liberty of final decision" (CC, Aug. 19, 1890).

Gilder had reservations about the theme of the novel, which
treats Christian Science in something less than respectful terms.
Knowing full well that the magazine would feel the brunt of the
outraged sensibilities produced by the novel among Christian Sci-
entists, he wanted to publish it anyway. Eggleston's assertions of
independence notwithstanding, Gilder's resolution to publish the
book took courage.

During the twenty-one years between Eggleston's first story

and *The Faith Doctor*, Eggleston's last extensive work of fiction, no one had a more significant direct influence upon Eggleston's writing than Gilder. It was Gilder who first persuaded Eggleston to write mature fiction, and it was Gilder who published virtually all of Eggleston's works beyond what was written for magazines edited by Eggleston himself. Yet Gilder had much less influence on Eggleston than he had upon any other American writer for his magazine. As an editor, Gilder could demand that writers who had no clear idea of what constituted a short story achieve a certain standard before he would accept their work. If their stories did not measure up to the standard, he could, and in many cases did, advise the author what steps might be taken to improve them. Eggleston's case was entirely different. When his first stories appeared in *Scribner's Monthly*, Eggleston, Gilder, and the magazine were all relatively untried. Even then, Eggleston had more training in writing than did such writers as Joel Chandler Harris, Thomas Nelson Page, or George W. Cable when their first stories appeared under Gilder's editorship. Also, the magazine itself was relatively fresh and uncluttered with other manuscripts in competition with Eggleston's. And, of course, Gilder was not the editor in 1871 that he was in 1881.

These factors combined to give Eggleston his start in fiction without much more than Gilder's passive help. During the second stage of his career, he achieved a certain prominence independent of Gilder. By the time he submitted *Roxy* to *Scribner's Monthly*, his reputation had grown far beyond his ability, and he was blessed with a seller's market for his fiction. As a result, he could demand and receive more editorial autonomy than most writers of the period.

That is not to say that had the situation been different Gilder could have raised the level of Eggleston's writing. No editor during Gilder's lifetime demanded that "magazine fiction" be raised to the level of literature before he would accept it. Eggleston acquired a polish and fluency in his writing that was adequate to his purposes and satisfactory to Gilder. If Eggleston's fiction had not matured independently, Gilder's editorial help probably would have been limited to the achievement of just that degree of polish that Eggleston acquired through self-criticism.

Something more than the businesslike editor-author relationship would have been needed if Gilder's influence on Eggleston were to have been more profound. Yet, despite innumerable contacts through sundry clubs and organizations, membership in the same social and literary circles, and great mutual respect, their relationship never really ripened into anything approaching a true friendship. Eggleston himself, reviewing his years in "the busy life of New York" from the vantage point of his retirement, spoke of his "long acquaintance and association" with Gilder, congratulating him "on the good influence [he exerts] in so many directions" (GP, Feb. 22, 1899). His choice of the words "acquaintance and association" is revealing; their relationship simply never achieved the intensity of the kind Gilder shared with Cable or Mark Twain.

II *Hamlin Garland*

Hamlin Garland's relationship with Gilder was quite the opposite of Eggleston's. Where Gilder "seduced" Eggleston to write for an untried, unestablished magazine, Garland supplicated the editor of one of the most powerful vehicles of American fiction to accept his work; where Eggleston for the most part refused editorial advice, Garland was influenced by Gilder's editorial advice to modify details in the stories he submitted to *The Century* and even, according to some modern critics, to revise his entire outlook on the purpose of fiction.[3]

Garland broke into *The Century* on his first attempt. In June, 1889, he sent three stories to Gilder with an apology for "bombarding [him] at wholesale." He asked Gilder to read the stories "with a due regard to the aims of the author," who aspired to give true representation of western life by dealing "not with abnormal phases so much as with representative phases." He assured Gilder that he was "western born," and that "the dialect and descriptive matter can be relied upon."[4] Gilder accepted one of the stories, "A Spring Romance," and paid Garland seventy-five dollars for it, the most money Garland had ever received for a story. Many years later, in *A Son of the Middle Border*, Garland described his feelings about this early success: "It meant something to get into the *Century* in those days. The praise of its editor was equivalent to a diploma. I regarded Gilder as second only to Howells in all that had to do with the judgment of fiction."[5]

Having established the precedent of one accepted story, Garland lost little time exploiting the new market that had opened to

him. He must have had a considerable stock of unpublished stories on hand, for his next shipment to Gilder was only three
months later. The letter accompanying the stories clearly stated his
willingness to revise the stories if Gilder thought revision was necessary, while emphasizing again his aim of fidelity to a true picture of "that Dakota life" (GC, Sept. 7, 1889). Gilder refused one
story, "A Prairie Heroine," and accepted the other, "Ol' Pap's
Flaxen." Gilder included a detailed criticism of "A Prairie Heroine" in his letter to Garland, a criticism of points so deeply embed-
ded in the story that there was no question of Garland's revising
and resubmitting the work. His criticisms were all aimed at examples of too-obvious didactic purpose, and Garland admitted the
validity of his criticisms, at least to a degree. "All you say is very
true," Garland wrote Gilder in return. "'Prairie Heroine' in some
phases is a little too obviously preaching." He approved of Gilder's concept about how didactic art ought to "present things con-
cretely and let others find the preaching." He concluded with Gilder that he had gone too far in his statement of the case of the
"toiling men and women" of the story (GC, Oct. 10, 1889).

In the case of "Ol' Pap's Flaxen," Garland was only too glad
to make the minor changes Gilder wanted. The story had been
refused by three other editors before Gilder accepted it, and Garland was eager to accept Gilder's criticisms of it. As he wrote Gilder, "I am always ready to accede to reasonable requests regarding my M.S.S. and I know that you would ask *only* [italics his]
the reasonable" (GC, n.d.). Unfortunately, because of the great
backlog of manuscripts in the files of *The Century*, Garland had
to wait two years before "Ol' Pap's Flaxen" appeared in the magazine. Although it was unlikely that Gilder would accept more of
his writings while the story remained unpublished, Garland per-
severed by sending Gilder first his play, "Under the Wheel,"
which Gilder rejected, and then the story, "A Girl of Modern
Tyre."

This last story is typical of Garland's realism and midwestern
local color. It is about a second-year college student, Albert Lohr,
who has dreams of a career in law and politics. At the time of the
story, he is working as a subscription book salesman with a gross
professional salesman, Jim Hartley, in a small midwestern town in
order to support himself during his next college year. He meets

Maud Welsh, who has been forced out of college because of family obligations. When they become so closely attached that neither can bear the thought of leaving the other, Albert regretfully abandons his career to marry her. The relationship is quite subtly drawn, and the idea of social pressure is developed very clearly.

Documentation of the progress of the story is unusually complete. The letters exchanged between Gilder and Garland about it illustrate in extraordinary detail some of the difficulties and rapprochements encountered and achieved by the story's western, socially oriented author, and its eastern, artistically oriented editor. They present a microcosm of Gilder's capacities and difficulties with realistic fiction and need little commentary. The first is Gilder's letter of acceptance of the story, qualified by his bewilderment over its purpose:

March 31, 1890

My dear Mr. Garland:

We have almost accepted "A Girl in Modern Tyre", but I can't seem to make out its meaning at all. So here it is again! You say I will like it because of its "purely artistic aim"; but after all I think I believe more in artistic treatment than in "artistic aim," except that a person should aim to do a thing well that he undertakes to do at all.

The story seems to have a special meaning, but what is it? Is it that the young man should not get married when half way through his college course, or that he should? Has he done a wrong thing or a right thing? You say "his dreams." Well,—he dreams of going to Congress. Why shouldn't he be a teacher, a lawyer, a politician, a Congressman, in the town where he has made so good a start? There is no earthly reason why he should not that I can see. "The sweet child eyes" might call him away from college, possibly, but not from the career which would lead to Congress; and then I don't see why he shouldn't simply have postponed his marriage and gone through college. Nothing to hinder that if the girl is the right sort of girl!

Yours sincerely,
R. W. Gilder [6]

Gilder's confusion was probably typical of eastern editors when confronted with hopelessness, one of the new motifs of western fiction, combined with certain elements of character equally new.

Garland attempted to clear up his confusion and explain the point
of the story:

MY DEAR GILDER:

My story is a "chunk o' life." I don't know why he can't go to
Congress—except that when love came to him it weakened him.
He wasn't strong enough anyway to fight for such leading posi-
tions as the West offered.

But the aim of the story is to set forth a common case of western
ambition. A river lost in sands. Out of twenty fine fellows who
started with me, fellows of equal or greater powers of grappling
and holding, seventeen are settled as Albert Lohr is settled in
those dead-and-alive western villages, as pettifogging lawyers,
principals of schools, or shop-keepers, I saw fifty bright fellows (at the very least fifty) during my six years of Seminary
life drop out and down as Albert did. Growing at length indiffer-
ent and in a way content with husks to fill their bellies. In a general way the story is a comment upon the all-pervading poverty
and barrenness of western life. Specifically it is a presentation (in
the best manner of the writer) of a bit of real life—of Albert Lohr,
a typical case.

Now I am ready to listen to suggestions. Can it be made fit for
your uses by changes here and there? If you are free to say I shall
be very glad to consider. I know it must appeal to you. There are
certain subtleties of treatment which I felt sure would please you.
Notably the handling of the boy in the last chapter and the character of Hartley. [sic]—which my brother counts one of the best.

In re-reading your letter I see one or two questions more. Why
can't he become a Congressman, etc. He *may* but the chances
are "agin him." Why didn't he postpone the marriage? Well, for
one thing, he was acting under the impulse that makes run-away
marriages sometimes. And second he saw that if he were to begin married life within a year, it would be worse than folly to
leave the girl to struggle there alone, while he spent all the money
he had and wasted a year in study which should be used in earn-
ing money.

I'm afraid you don't know the drear hopelessness of a small
country town, especially in the West, as well as I do. What he
would be most likely to do would be to *go West*. Almost never
would such a man look East.

Let me have a further word with you.

                                                Sincerely,
                                                HAMLIN GARLAND

I can easily put the ideas I have written you into the story in explanation.

Oblige me with an early note, won't you?

H. G.[7]

Gilder did oblige with a letter which, after acknowledging Garland's explanation, dwelt at length on a point which Garland said later "revealed the heart of his editorial policy." [8] Actually, as the full correspondence reveals, it was only one of a series of points made in connection with this story:

April 5, 1890

My dear Mr. Garland:

I think if, without making the story too inartistically pointed, you could get in those ideas which you have expressed to me in your letter, it would dignify and make more useful the really very striking picture of life which you have presented. If you will do this and let me see the story again, I shall be greatly obliged to you.

I must tell you what embarrasses me in stories of this sort. As you know, the newspaper press now-a-days is vulgarizing. It not only expresses the vulgarity of the American masses, but increases it,—that is, to a large extent. Every decent man and woman including many newspaper men deprecates this condition of things. Now if we print too many stories which are full of the kind of language which should not be used, we seem to many persons to be continuing the work of vulgarization. On the other hand, we value correct pictures of life—and the consequence is we are giving an undue proportion, possibly, of dialect fiction. People who are trying to bring up their children with refinement, and to keep their own and their children's language pure and clean, very naturally are jealous of the influence of the magazine,—especially of the Century Magazine,—in this respect. Here is really a predicament, and feeling that predicament, we at least think a dialect story,—especially of this kind, where "yup" is used for yes, for instance, and where all sorts of vulgarisms occur,—should very strongly recommend itself before being sent into almost every cultivated household in the United States! Had you thought of the matter in this connection? I am very far from wishing to go to an extreme in the other direction—lords and ladies—but I think we should not go to an extreme in this direction.

Sincerely,

R. W. Gilder[9]

Garland replied with a complete agreement about Gilder's ideas on language and promised correction of the manuscript along the lines suggested by Gilder:

DEAR MR. GILDER:

There is this saving clause about dialect (though parents may never think of it). It is *usually* spoken by one whom the child reading feels is illiterate and not to be copied. I believe in general that *dialect* does not corrupt a child so much as "highfalutin language." The child says to itself, "this man talks funny. The writer knows he talks funny. I mustn't talk as he does."

Practically any one capable of reading my work would feel precisely this way. The only possible danger of corruption of language which could come from good dialect writings is in occasionally letting a really fine thoughtful fellow like Albert Lohr say "Yup" for yes. But this I think you and I realize is not at all a great danger.

Our great trouble today over "corrupting" of the language of youth as you indicated in your note springs more from the infernal conglomerate, stilted, vulgar conventional "newspaper English" which is not graphic, dignified nor characteristic. I think the language of the common people is beautiful, pictorial and splendidly dramatic beside it.

I feel that we are not far apart on these things. I *love* the language of the farmer and the mechanic so swift sure and direct, but I loathe the reporter's diction and the diction of the country newspaper. I intend using it but in the way of ridicule, to help drive it out. However, I feel the pressure which is brought to bear upon you on these lines, and I am perfectly willing to make compromises to make your predicament less vexatious. I feel that you would not ask me to sacrifice unnecessarily and I think you must know me well enough to know that everything I do has *lift* in it—that I want to bring beauty and comfort and intelligence into the common American home. All I write or do has that underlying purpose.

I shall therefore soften down the lingual sins of Albert. I don't think there is danger from the dialect of Hartley—because they will see that *he* is not the principal personage, not the one having the author's complete sympathy. The other suggestions I will carry out and return the m.s. soon.

Sincerely,

HAMLIN GARLAND (GC [Apr. 7, 1890])

Garland made the corrections and returned the manuscript in less than a month. His corrections were so thorough that Gilder did not feel it necessary to return the manuscript to him with suggestions for the few other changes he wanted. Instead, he merely called nine points to Garland's attention:

May 7th, 1890

MY DEAR GARLAND:

Many thanks for your revision of "A Girl in Modern Tyre."

I don't know that it is necessary to send back the copy, but I will tell you of some things which I hope you will consent to.

(1) Would you mind substituting, say, Grant's book for Blaine's. The name of Blaine brings up such violent and disagreeable controversies, and it runs all through the story.

(2) In the first part there are one or two places where the conversation is stretched out to an unnecessary extent and I have struck them out. In sending the final proofs we can send you the copy too, showing you where it is. It is only in two places. The first omission occurs here:

"Over there" was the surly reply.

"How far?"

" 'Bout a mile."

"A mile?"

"That's what 'a said, a mile."

"Well I'll be blanked!"

"Well y' better be doing something besides standing here, 'r y'll freeze t' death. I'd go over to the Arteeshun House an' go t' bed if I was in your fix."

"The Artesian is owned by the railway, eh?"

"Yup."

"And you're the clerk?"

"Yup. Nice little scheme aint it?"

The part omitted is between the lines "if I was in your fix" and "The Arteeshun is owned by the railway, eh?" This omitted part is unnecessary and seems to me to weaken it; as, "Well where is the Artesian House" etc.

In another place I have struck out some unnecessary conversation in the hotel on the lamp, beginning with "Spit on it" to "Sufficient unto the day is the evil thereof." Plenty is left to keep the local color.

(3) You call one of the lamps "horrible little." Is not that too strong a word? Why not "absurd little."

(4) Again page 3, I have written Vanderbilt in the place of Jay Gould. Jay Gould is a live thief whom we would rather not honor, even in that way.

Page 13, you say "sat down at the organ and played a gospel hymn or two from the Moody and Sanky hymnal, infallibly in such homes." The words "infallibly in such homes" are unnecessary and weaken the statement. When you introduce a Moody and Sanky hymnal there you do it because it is "infallibly in such homes" and it seems to me inartistic to add the definite statement.

(5) Page 28, I can't make out this line. "Hartley came in a few moments later and found Bert sitting thoughtfully by the fire with his coat and shoes off—evidently in deep abstraction." "We'll rag at away at last—much as ever." What is this last line.

(6) Page 53, you say of Brann, "The struggle had been pro-digious, but he had snatched defeat out of victory." You mean "victory out of defeat," don't you? You add "His better nature had conquered."

(7) The story should end without the few last words, I think, because they are a repetition, and perhaps a little bit sordid too. It closes more naturally "Three pairs of sweet childish eyes held him prisoner—though a willing one." I struck out the following: "Certain of his dreams must ever remain dreams. Over his head the heights of wealth and power lift each year growing more in-accessible to him and all like him." This idea is in just before, and its repetition weakens the close.

Sincerely,
R. W. GILDER

Many thanks for your photograph. I see you sign it "for single tax." But are you not in favor of international copyright, the Ser-mon on the Mount, and summer vacations?" [10]

Garland accepted Gilder's criticisms in general, but he was ap-parently a little miffed at the *esprit* of Gilder's postscript, which he countered with a certain amount of seriousness:

DEAR GILDER:
Your letter at hand. Glad the tale needs so little cutting. Criti-cisms accepted. "Horrible little lamp" meant its *odor*. "Horribly smelling" should be the words. Blaine's book seems necessary for the fun—or at least it ought to be *partisan*. We can use any name we please, "Thompson" or "Smith's fifty years in Congress." I didn't mean to be exact. There's such a delicious bit—Hartley's giving such a book to Mrs. Welsh—and proposing a morocco

copy for Maud! It wants to be a book that *some* people wouldn't touch with tongs. I think we can get around that with some other name.

Yes I believe in the Single-Tax and "the Single-tax" with me means international copy-right, the Sermon on the Mount and Summer Vacations for everybody. But why didn't you send your photo. I want to have a presentment of the Editor who first measured my work.

> Sincerely yours,
> HAMLIN GARLAND (GC. [after May 7, 1890])

Garland continued as an occasional contributor to *The Century* after the publication of this story and as a friend of Gilder's through the latter's life, but those contacts were a mere epilogue and anticlimax to the relationship we have described. To understand Gilder's influence on Garland and to see Gilder as an editor of western fiction, we need only analyze their relationship in 1889 and 1890. The analysis produces several points of great importance.

First, as Donald Pizer has pointed out in *Hamlin Garland's Early Work and Career,* Gilder did not attempt to turn Garland away from writing stories of social protest, as some modern critics have claimed. These critics cite as evidence of Gilder's emasculating influence Garland's own statements in several places that Gilder was among those who advised him not to be carried away by his social enthusiasms. But Gilder's advice, judging from the record of his editorial letters, was obviously based more on a thorough awareness of what constitutes literary effectiveness than from any tendency to shrink from truth. As Gilder put it, he believed more in "artistic treatment than in 'artistic aim.' "

Two incidents in the correspondence relating to "A Girl of Modern Tyre" bear out this interpretation of Gilder's editorial judgment. When Gilder found it difficult to understand the point of the story, he asked Garland, in effect, to explain its social significance. Then, even though Garland's explanation was to point out the "all-pervading poverty and barrenness," as well as the "drear hopelessness" of life in the West, Gilder requested that Garland add these explanations to the story to make his position clearer. This point is most significant. Gilder had already refused works by Garland (as we have seen he did also with Cable) because they were "too obviously preaching," yet he requests the

same author to "preach," to draw conclusions or point out underlying purposes that he felt had not been clearly formulated. No
more convincing evidence could be found to prove that Gilder's
purpose was entirely to increase the literary effect of Garland's
work and not merely to have it conform to the standards of the
"genteel tradition."

Again, after Garland had "softened down the lingual sins of
Albert," Gilder's specific requests for revisions (in the letter of
May 7, 1890) were intended, with only two exceptions, to increase
the effectiveness of Garland's social commentary. Revisions num-
bered two, three, the second part of four, five, six, and seven are
all either proofreader's questions; suggestions for the elimination
of repetitive dialogue; or, in the case of question four, part two,
requests for the elimination of an inartistic conclusion. Of the two
exceptions, question one reveals Gilder's personal bias against
James G. Blaine, and question four, part one, is intended to
avoid libel suits. Still, Gilder's statement that Jay Gould was a
"live thief" shows that he was sympathetic with Garland's treatment of Gould. But these are minor points at best, and we can
only conclude that Gilder's editing was directed almost entirely at
sharpening Garland's style and at giving point to his conclusions,
both proper editorial functions.

If Gilder did not directly advise Garland against writing works
of social protest, did he indirectly force him to soften his material
by rejecting strong works of that character? To argue that point is
to give too much credit to *The Century Magazine*. Garland could
and did take his works elsewhere after Gilder had refused them.
Gilder, on the other hand, had commitments to his subscribers
that could not be ignored. And, while he published none of Garland's stronger stories, he was the first editor of a major monthly
to publish *any* of Garland's work; and, what is more significant,
several of the stories he published had been rejected by other
monthlies before Gilder accepted them.

Though Gilder was not a radical, either in his social thought or
in his editing, it is obvious that he worked to help Garland in the
only way he could: by publishing any and all stories which, as he
put it, did not "unduly shock or distress the readers of the magazine which does not intend to be a battleground of opinion." If
Garland saw fit to water down his fiction to make it correspond to
what he considered Gilder's standards, that was his own decision.

The fact that he apparently produced both literature of social protest and lighter literature concurrently—that he could mail "A Prairie Heroine" and "Ol' Pap's Flaxen" to Gilder in the same package—proves that there was no such irreconcilable choice involved.

In general, Gilder seems hardly to have been a corrupting influence upon Garland. He was the first important editor to give Garland that most significant of gratifications for the young writer, the acceptance of a story. If he refused others, he accepted many; and he was willing to examine all fairly. As Garland said of him, Gilder "lived in the constant hope of discovering genius in every mail." [11] If he demanded some revisions of slang and "profanity," he allowed Garland to keep enough dialect to reflect accurately the local color he wanted to achieve. If he objected to didacticism, he was also willing to have Garland point out the "drear hopelessness" of life in the West when he felt the moral had not been made clear enough. If he pleaded for some beauty in a story, he also was willing to face a certain amount of unpleasantness. In short, he was as receptive to the new techniques and the new social consciousness of western writers as his responsibilities to his subscribers would permit.

If we consider Gilder's relationship with both Eggleston and Garland, we are led to some further conclusions about Gilder's treatment of western fiction. In the first place, there can be no doubt that Gilder found it easier to accept the softer, more sentimental, descriptive local color of Eggleston than he did the more socially oriented, bleaker "veritism" of Hamlin Garland. While Gilder was more receptive to the work of both men than was any other important eastern editor, it is nonetheless true that the later forms of the genre of realistic writing were unacceptable to him.

The range and growth of Gilder's tolerance for realistic fiction may be deduced from his acceptance of two of the stories considered above. Eggleston's "The Gunpowder Plot" suggests the primitive conditions of life on the Wisconsin frontier—the drunken release of civilized inhibitions by the trappers, the bleak loneliness of Lindsley's farm—without emphasizing the social evils involved. Eggleston sought no farther than a love interest to make all right again. "A Girl of Modern Tyre," on the other hand, points out truthfully, though never brutally, several facts of life in the Midwest, from the physical hardships of the weather to the stresses placed on youth by emotions and situations which are less damning to ambition in the East. These two stories represent Gilder's range in local color; significantly, it could never include *Jason Edwards* or "A Prairie Heroine," in which the degradation of life in the West is clearly stated and the social causes are made evident. Certainly Gilder had his limitations; and, in attempting to show that they were not so narrowly drawn as some critics have suggested, I would not want to suggest that they were not present at all.

One of the reasons for Gilder's incapacity to accept more violent western stories of social protest was his almost complete ignorance of the conditions of life in the West and his inability to understand the new motifs of fiction from that section. His letter of March 31, 1890, to Garland is remarkable evidence of that incapacity. "I'm afraid you don't know the drear hopelessness of a small country town, especially in the West, as well as I do," replied Garland, and surely he was right. Had Gilder been able to see "a piece of the great West," as he wanted, it would not have helped. His childhood, his education, his work, his social milieu, all the elements that shaped his esthetic were eastern and urban. Necessarily his sympathy with western problems was as limited as his understanding of them.

This conclusion is supported by a comparison of Gilder's relations with the writers of that other great area from which *Scribner's Monthly* and *The Century* drew fiction, the South. Gilder was able to sympathize with Cable's ideas about the Negro much more than he could with Garland's ideas about the western farmer, for to him the southern question was more clearly one of the implementation of ideals. The Negro had what Gilder saw as right and justice on his side, right and justice which were being denied him by a clearly defined social group. The western farmer, on the other hand, was in Gilder's eyes western and a farmer by choice, and protested only against that most ill-defined of malevolences, "conditions." "I don't see why [Albert] shouldn't simply have postponed his marriage and gone through college," Gilder wrote, revealing his inability to understand social compulsion. If Garland could have produced a villain—a well-defined and unquestionable reason for the degradation of the farmer in the West —Gilder's reaction would have been totally different. But the complexity of the situation and his own social and economic naïveté combined to make him incapable of direct action in the situation as it was.

That, briefly, is the case against Gilder as an editor of western fiction. That these limitations were not totally damning to his success as an editor may best be seen by an examination, more detailed than any we have yet considered, of his relationship with two of the most important writers of his day, William Dean Howells and Mark Twain. Both men were from the West, and both gave Gilder opportunities to prove himself perhaps the most capable magazine editor of his century.

CHAPTER *6*

William Dean Howells

WE HAVE seen Gilder the poet-editor, Gilder the liberal in relation to the Negro question, and Gilder the champion of American writers. In the process we seem to have left behind in the first chapter the Gilder who was an exceedingly competent editor. There is no better way to redress this omission than by a consideration of Gilder's career vis-à-vis that of William Dean Howells. Their careers are remarkably similar, Howells standing as an *a fortiori* to Gilder's standard. Seven years older than Gilder, Howells lived eleven years longer. Gilder's sixteen volumes of poetry would stand like a footnote to Howells' eighty-odd volumes of prose and poetry (not counting plays). If Gilder discovered his dozens of new writers, Howells found his in gross lots. If Gilder's critical notions taught writers to "be bold, be bold, be not too bold," Howells taught them to "be bolder, bolder—but not too much bolder." In short, Howells was everything Gilder was and something more—but certainly not so much more as the disparity in their reputations today would suggest.

They started out approximately as equals in 1871. Howells had moved eastward and upward from a print shop in Hamilton, Ohio, to the editorship of *The Atlantic Monthly* in Boston. Gilder made a shorter, but no less steep, journey from Bordentown, New Jersey, to *Scribner's Monthly*. Howells' route included peregrinations abroad, while Gilder had crossed no bodies of water larger than the Hudson; but, as heir-apparent to Holland, his prospects were surely as bright as Howells' at that moment. During the decade of the 1870's their careers continued to run parallel, the one in Boston, the other in New York. Howells engaged in a feud of sorts with Holland, but his relations with Gilder were always cordial. Indeed, he invited Gilder to contribute some poetry to *The Atlantic;* and, though Gilder could not comply with his request, he told Howells that he would consider it "a high honor to appear . . . in any magazine" edited by Howells.[1] What little contact they had during this decade was that of like minds and talents several hundred miles apart, only occasionally cooperating actively, even more rarely in competition with each other. Probably they would have continued thus had not Howells left *The Atlantic* in 1880 and had not Gilder become editor in name as well as in fact of *The Century Magazine*. At that point their fortunes crossed and remained intertwined until Howells went to work for *Harper's* in 1885.

Unbound to any magazine for editorial or creative work, Howells had his pick of American and English magazines in which to publish his fiction during those years from 1880 to 1885, but the great majority of his work during these years was published by Gilder. Fifteen of Howells' twenty-nine periodical contributions, including four of five novels, appeared in *Scribner's Monthly* and *The Century*. Obviously, Howells found in Gilder an appreciation for his work and an editorial capacity that helped to make this period the most creative one of his life.

I *Gilder's "Fearful Responsibility"*

Howells' first contribution to Gilder's magazine, the short novel *A Fearful Responsibility,* produced more disagreements and difficulties between the two men than all the rest put together. Throughout the period when the story was being written and prepared for publication in the magazine, Howells was as testy and difficult as a prima donna; but Gilder's politesse was never more evident. Howells showed every indication of distrust in his new editor; Gilder, every indication of an unwillingness to alienate Howells.

Gilder first wrote Howells that the story could be started in the May, 1881, number and could have twelve pages of 850 words each, adding, "I need not say how delighted we all are at the prospect of getting it at all" (HP, Mar. 8, 1881). Howells replied that twelve pages would not be enough and that he could not finish the installment in time for the May issue. Gilder wrote protesting—gently, very gently—the latter point: "Pardon an editorial importunity, but we ripped apart the May number to get the beginning of the story in & can't give up the idea of having it there. This number is one of the four special numbers of the year

—has a frontispiece . . . and begins a volume. We have still further despoiled the No. in order to let in say fifteen pages for you & we sincerely hope that without too much friction you can come up to the scratch" (HP, Mar. 12, 1881).

The May issue was put together again, without Howells' story; and, in a letter dated March 26, Gilder asked for copy for June. By March 31, he had received it; and he wrote Howells then and again on April 5 praising its "healthy vivacity and interest," and calling it "a great acquisition to the magazine!" But, writing about where the breaks in the narrative were to occur, Gilder by a slip of the pen promised to get all of the story to the end of "part VII" into the first installment; Howells had asked to have the break occur after Part VI. When Howells complained vehemently about this contretemps, Gilder used the opportunity to soothe his new contributor with a long letter that says a great deal about two points of paramount interest to this study—the problems of magazine publishing in general, and Gilder's eagerness to keep Howells content.

April 21st, 1881

MY DEAR MR. HOWELLS:

I am distressed to find that you misunderstood what we said about this first installment. If I said the "7th division" was to be included it was a slip of the pen. I meant division VI. At first not knowing the length of the story—we thought we could get along with what we first sent to you. Then finding the story would be longer than we supposed, and that you still wished it all to appear in two numbers, we added four magazine pages to this first installment and promised to add still further divisions if we learned by cable that there was danger of the Revised New Testament being postponed.[2] Our London telegram was an assurance that there would be no postponement, and so we had to use Professor Fisher's article—for which we had been preparing for months if not for years. We meantime omitted all that was possible from the editorial pages. You see the matter of illustration & the necessity of roughing out the numbers months, and even years, in advance makes it less feasible to do just what we would like to at the last moment.

In getting a story as long as this into two numbers we are doing what we have never done before; and this scheme coming late into our plans makes a pressure inconceivable to any one not inside. We felt the candle is worth the game, however, & are anx-

ious, moreover, to meet your own & Mr. Osgood's wishes without
regard to physical considerations.

As it stands now although we would prefer letting the story run
into a third number—we feel that your own judgment as to the
effect of three rather than two installments is something that we
cannot set ourselves against—for you are both an author & an
editor. We fear, however, there is danger of your modestly under-
estimating the interest, & the divisable "eligibility" (as Walt
Whitman would barbarously say) of the story. However it is a
fearful responsibility for us to suggest its cutting up in three—
& we therefore engage to print, if you wish, the whole remaining part in the July number. Will you not, then, kindly let us have
copy as soon as possible—it should all be in the printer's hands
by this time.

Faithfully,
R. W. GILDER (HP)

Howells' concern over the editorial treatment of this story
stands unique in his relationship with Gilder and *Scribner's
Monthly* and *The Century*. There were no comparable difficulties
connected with any other of his publications in the magazine, and
eventually his willingness to accept Gilder's editorial importuni-
ties became almost a legend in *The Century's* offices. The reason
for his sensitivity is, I believe, probably because of Josiah Holland's continuing position as titular head of the magazine, even
though it should have been apparent to anyone by 1880 that Gilder was the magazine's real guiding force. But, by the time
Howells' next contribution was published, Gilder had become sole
editor of the magazine upon the death of Holland.

Even before *A Fearful Responsibility* was published, Gilder
was working to draw more material from Howells. As early as
March 12, 1881, he asked Howells for "some ideal illustrated article." A few weeks later he followed the request with an admoni-
tion: "As to an illustratable article we would like to have some
suggestions from you: not something in 'our line'—we would
rather improve upon 'our line' than imitate it" (HP, Mar. 26,
1881). Gilder next asked if it would be agreeable for Howells "to
notice some work in which you are particularly interested," and
then apostrophized: "The old cities of Italy! How would they do
for an illustrated series? . . . Verona—Padua—Siena—Perugia"
(HP, Apr. 5, 1881). The suggestion struck a responsive chord, and

Howells agreed to a contract for the series, subject to his going to Italy.

Gilder was apparently willing to print all of Howells' work and still urge him to do more. His suggestions to Howells for publishable possibilities were so many and various that he even parodied his own eagerness with a suggestion that Howells write an essay on life "behind the scenes" at a flea circus (HP, May 9, 1881). A few day later he took a more positive viewpoint. Answering some misgivings of Howells about taking on too much new work, Gilder wrote, "No,—I don't think there is any danger from magnificent conceptions. I only wonder that the release from editorial bondage has not produced about twenty thousand magnificent projects instead of only a half dozen or so" (HP, May 14, 1881). The letters of both men at this period are positively euphoric. Howells was feeling the intense pleasure of eager delight on the part of a sympathetic, intelligent editor; Gilder, for his part, seems to have been enjoying vicariously the pleasures which Howells experienced in freedom from editorial work. Viewed from either side, the situation was stimulating, electric. It should be no surprise that it enabled Howells to produce some of his best work.

The fruits of this collaboration took two forms—Howells' critical articles on Twain and James (published in *The Century* in September and November, 1882) and the first of Howells' four serial novels for *The Century, A Modern Instance*. This novel produced for its author and for the magazine in which it was serialized one of the greatest commercial and artistic successes in nineteenth-century American fiction. The history of the publication of *A Modern Instance* includes none of the difficulties that beset Gilder and Howells over *A Fearful Responsibility*. The most important problem confronting the two men seems to have been merely the choice of a title.

As was his usual custom, Howells submitted a list of eleven titles to Gilder. At first, both men seemed to favor "A New Medea"; and, as late as August 15, Gilder thought the matter was settled. Howells had reservations about that title, however, and asked Gilder to consider the alternatives further. The question dragged on for two months. Gilder resolutely refused to make the final choice, although he was willing to narrow the field somewhat:

"A New Medea" seems to me the best. I always come back to that. But if I knew the story better I might find something jarring in the name, as applied. . . . "Stony Ground" is not bad. "An American Situation" I don't take to at all; it seems to carry a sort of aspersion in it. "A Married Life" perhaps gives away the plot less than the Medea title—& it is otherwise reticent. "Marcia Hubbard's Marriage" is not objectionable—but it seems to belong rather to a short story. . . . I wouldn't have a "Commonplace Histy [History]," I think; it is not so good as "Annals of a Quiet Neighborhood" and is too deprecatory for a title running a whole year—isn't it.

Wish I had more firm convictions on the subject, but all the eleven titles are interesting. Suppose you write us short stories for the ten discarded titles. (HP, Sept. 9, 1881)

A month later Gilder again refused to take the responsibility for the choice of a title: "It is impossible for me to be of much use to you in this matter as I don't know the story." Then, only five days later, he apparently had an inspiration, for his letter opens, " 'Marcia' a Modern Tragedy. How does this strike you" (HP, Oct. 8, 1881). This suggestion is still quite a distance from *A Modern Instance*, but it is likely that it triggered the associative process that produced the final title. At any rate, the naming of the novel is not mentioned again.

Perhaps the most significant element in this interchange about the title of the novel is the fact that it represents virtually all of the correspondence of this period. The bickering over "A Fearful Responsibility" was past, even though Gilder made requests of Howells not once, but *twice* that would have provoked anguished outcries had they been made about the earlier story. Some verbal changes were made by editorial proofreaders of the novel with no protest on Howells' part, and a different beginning date was suggested, a circumstance that Howells had objected to strenuously when it had occurred in relation to the earlier story.[3] These were, after all, minor matters to two men who may very well have been in a haze of pleasure—pleasure, on the one hand, of work sincerely appreciated; pleasure, on the other, of vicarious identification.

II *Euphoria*

The period during which A *Modern Instance* was serialized in *The Century* was one of continuous growth for the magazine, both popular and artistic. Gilder had executed an editorial coup by garnering for his magazine the finest novel yet produced by Howells. From a distance of eighty years it is possible to forget, on the one hand, how difficult this coup was and, on the other, how significant a triumph it was in terms of the magazine's continued success.[4] Both points are important as indications of Gilder's competence as an editor and as evidence that Howells' trust in him was not misplaced.

The difficulty involved in acquiring a novel like A *Modern Instance* for *The Century* totally contradicts the current image of Gilder as a conservative editor, hag-ridden by "genteel" morality. It is well known that Howells' custom in writing his novels was to outline the plot, estimate the length of the completed work, and then sell the outlined work to a magazine for serialization. As we have seen in the case of Mrs. Burnett's serialization of *Through One Administration,* mentioned in Chapter One, such a method of composition was, for the editor, fraught with dangerous possibilities, including the chance of delays, incorrect estimates about the length of installments and of the complete work, and, of course, most frightening of all, turns of plot and situation "unsuitable for the audience of a family magazine."

Gilder had confidence in Howells' literary capabilities and good taste. He felt that, since Howells was "both an author and an editor," he could be trusted to exhibit both esthetic and moral responsibility consistently in his writing. Every contract given Howells for publications in *The Century* reflects this confidence. When Roswell Smith confirmed the contract for A *Woman's Reason,* for example, he wrote Osgood that "Gilder does not wish to read the MS unless he can do Mr. Howells a service in doing so" (HP, Jan. 2, 1882). The Italian sketches and *The Rise of Silas Lapham* were accepted under similar conditions—or, rather, lack of them.

In spite of all this confidence in Howells, it should be remembered that the outline of A *Modern Instance* must have sketched the marital difficulties of the Hubbard family and certainly the importance of the question of divorce in the dénouement of the story. No matter how much confidence Gilder had in Howells' taste, the signing of a contract for an unwritten novel of the character of *A Modern Instance* required editorial courage. This editorial willingness to contract for as yet unwritten works allowed Gilder to acquire over three-fourths of Howells' output during the years Howells was not employed by *The Atlantic* or *Harper's.* Such editorial courage was not acquired by Henry Mills Alden of *Harper's,* for example, until long after Gilder had shown other magazine editors how fruitful faith in Howells' good taste could be. Alden, at this period, was still unwilling to accept works by Howells without the manuscript in hand.[5] It may be assumed that other editors shared his unwillingness and that Gilder's greater liberality was largely responsible for the high percentage of Howells' work published by *The Century* between 1881 and 1885.

Considering these circumstances and the immense success resultant upon Gilder's willingness to take what appears only retrospectively as a not very unsure gamble, it is perhaps excusable that Gilder allowed himself to gloat a bit over his triumph. It was partly the triumph and partly his sincere appreciation of Howells' work that prompted Gilder to write Howells halfway through the serialization of *A Modern Instance:* "You must know what an immense and strongly moved audience you are drawing along with you in this powerful story. It is success in every way, both as literature and as 'magazine literature.' The moral quality is both strong and artistic. One applauds with equal spontaneity the meaning and the method. This installment especially is weighted with moral criticism—and yet how dramatic" (HP, Mar. 27, 1882).

Substantially the same sentiments, particularly regarding the moral quality of the novel, were repeated by Gilder in an unsigned editorial in *The Century* entitled "Mr. Howells on Divorce." After noting that *The Century* had led the way to open discussions of the problems of marriage and divorce (a very difficult and unpopular topic in that day), Gilder pointed out the basic strength of *A Modern Instance* in terms that are still critically sound:

Mr. Howells's argument . . . applies to the individual conscience; it touches and lays bare the springs of human conduct; it holds up a mirror, not merely to the hopelessly selfish and impure heart, but to many others; for there is hardly a human soul bound by

sacred ties to another that might not be startled, warned, and
strengthened by the image he or she can find in this divining glass
fashioned by a true artist.

"Artist," we say, for if the author had forgotten his art under
the stress of his moral message, he would have been untrue, not
only to his own conscience, but to life. We doubt if Mr. Howells's
art was ever seen in greater perfection than in his latest work.[6]

Interest in the magazine was heightened by the appearance of
another controversial work by Howells in the November, 1882,
issue of *The Century*. In an article on Henry James that was a
manifesto for the new literature, Howells took dead aim at several
idols of English literature, saying, among other things, that "the
art of fiction has . . . become a finer art in our day than it was
with Dickens and Thackeray. We could not suffer the confidential
attitude of the latter now, nor the mannerism of the former, any
more than we could endure the prolixity of Richardson or the
coarseness of Fielding" (XXV, 28). Gilder was exultant about the
situation in a letter to Howells written December 16, 1882:

> The modern novel, and especially the American counterpart, is
> getting a pretty thorough overhauling—the "Tribune" publishes
> three or four editorials, paragraphs, or communications weekly on
> this subject. The new novel [*A Woman's Reason*] will come out
> in the midst of the talk . . . and will add fuel to the fire. It is the
> simultaneous appearance of the article on James and the serial by
> yourself (Modern Instance) that has made the buzz. Gosse was
> frightened at first . . . but he now feels that the Channel waters
> are not going to swamp us—and that our peak now stands up
> higher than before. It takes a good deal to frighten us here at
> home—with the subscriptions coming in well. (HP, Dec. 16,
> 1882)

The end of the year 1883 marked the high point in the relationship between Howells and Gilder, the end of a period of self-
congratulation and of a period in which all three parties involved
—Howells, Gilder, and the magazine (not to mention the American and English reading public)—derived mutual benefits. Gilder
was so pleased with Howells' contributions to the magazine that
he attempted to get him a chair of literature at the Johns Hopkins
University, but Howells refused the offer. The euphoria continued

through the publication of Howells' second novel for the magazine, *A Woman's Reason.*

III   *The Saturation Point*

With all the successes that the association of Howells and Gilder had produced, Gilder was forced by the end of 1883 to draw some lines about how far he could go, even with his most prized author. *The Century* had a saturation point for any author, and Gilder finally was forced to discourage Howells' contributions. During the years 1881–1882, Howells had contributed to twenty-two out of twenty-four issues of *The Century.* While *A Woman's Reason* was still running in the magazine (February–October, 1883), Howells was still under obligations to Gilder for a series of Italian sketches and one novel. Then, near the end of 1883, he asked to be commissioned for one or two more novels and a play. Gilder's replies were tactful but firm. *The Century* would consider a play to be published in a single number, but would not accept "a serial in that form." He then discussed the projected novel(s):

> I feel the loss of the novel and would have been all the more chagrined had it not been inevitable. But, as I understood it, here was the problem—after our announcements and plans for the present year were made—to print before the end of the year which begins next autumn—your travel papers—and three novels by you, or possibly only two, none of which were completed and some not begun, but all needing to be made into books by one year from next autumn. If the book publication could have been deferred we might have taken all—as it was it was impossible, and we *chose* with a view to variety of subject, and without the opportunity of seeing a line of manuscript. So don't tantalize a poor editor with the idea of a lost prize! [7]

Obviously, this letter reflects decisions made partly by the business office of the magazine which, at least in the case of the lost novel, Gilder sincerely regretted. His next refusal, of Howells' projected play, was his own decision, and it was brutally stated in his letter of December 27, 1883:

> After considerable thought and consultation we have come to the conclusion

1st that a *long* play, that is, of thirty or forty pages, would not
be desirable in the magazine

2nd that the magazine could not afford to pay for a play anything like the price asked

3rd that we would not be willing to experiment in this direction without having the opportunity to read the Ms. (GL)

One of the most curt letters Gilder ever wrote, this refusal to
Howells seems to have been prompted by repeated requests from
Howells on the three points considered. Gilder did not like to
print plays anyway (they rarely appeared in *The Century,* and
when they were published they were always short), and he believed that they did not evoke much reader interest because of
their form, whatever their content. Howells, he must have believed, was exploiting his connection with *The Century* to market
a genre of his writing with which he had not had much success
elsewhere. If this were the case, it would explain the curtness of
his letter.

These refusals hardly diminished the flow of manuscripts from
Howells. A suggestion from Gilder that Howells do some reviewing for the magazine produced reviews of John Hay's *The Breadwinners* and "Two Notable Novels"—a review of Edward Bel-
lamy's *Miss Ludington's Sister* and E. W. Howe's *The Story of a
Country Town.* At about the same time, Gilder contracted for six
of nine short stories by Howells, choosing from the titles alone;
and he voiced a hope that Howells would write one or two more
articles which could be suitably illustrated. And about this time
the interests of both men began to center on the novel that was to
run in *The Century* from November, 1884, to August, 1885, *The
Rise of Silas Lapham.*

The contract for this novel was agreed to in December, 1883. At
that time Howells submitted a synopsis of the novel as he imag-
ined it, then entitled "The Rise of Silas Needham," to Gilder,
along with a synopsis of *Indian Summer.* Gilder, as we have seen,
was forced to choose between the two. *Indian Summer* is a charming novel; but certainly no one would say that its plot, as it appeared in a synopsis, could cause even the most prudish reader
any qualms. *Silas Lapham,* on the other hand, even in a synopsis,
should have caused a "genteel" editor to shun it because the prob-

lem of business morality inevitably would be a touchy subject for a middle-class audience.[8] Gilder's decision, as we shall see, did not go unchallenged in the serialization, but was finally crowned with the success which the novel achieved.

All went well at first, once the decision to publish was made. Except for the change of "Lapham" for "Needham," there was no difficulty with the title, as there had been with *A Modern Instance*. Publication proceeded smoothly through the first installments of the novel. On January 3, 1885, Gilder wrote Howells his congratulations: "Silas Lapham is pronounced generally one of your strongest stories; the dinner scene is, of its kind, unsurpassed" (HP). Then, a month later, an incident occurred in relation to the same "dinner scene" that is singularly significant in terms of Gilder's editorial capacity. A letter he wrote to Howells on February 18, 1885, has been partially quoted by several critics as evidence of Gilder's editorial timidity:

MY DEAR MR. HOWELLS,

The leap made this year in the Century's circulation—up to 210,000 & *still rising*—has thrown upon us, we cannot help feeling, a greater responsibility than ever, & we cannot help being on guard against any false step which may injure our destiny and influence. A week or two ago we cancelled 150,000 pages [the press run] in an article by Mr. Bigelow[9] (with his consent) in which he quoted an enthusiastic endorsement of dynamite war-fare on the Parliament buildings and reigning houses generally. We had not objected to this while dynamiting was an insignificant matter; but with recent events before our eyes the paragraph had a new significance—it would doubtless have been copied by dynamite journals as an endorsement of their methods, and possibly might have led to the seizure of the magazine in England.

I hope you will not think us super-sensitive when we call your attention to page 867 of your April installment—where some words written months ago assume a new meaning in the light of new events. It is the very word *dynamite*, that is now so dangerous for any of us to use, except in condemnation. None but a crank would misinterpret your allusion, but it is the crank who does the deed. The other day it was found that dynamite had been built into all the hearths in a new house! There is no telling where this sort of thing is going to break out—it is an unknown and horribly inflammable quantity, and we don't want, if we can help it, to

be associated with the subject—except as opposing it. I am confident that on reflection you will take this view, and if so can you telegraph (and also write) a line or two to take the place of the phrase which introduces the word "dynamite." If you cannot make the matter clear (at our expense) by telegraph, then please telegraph that you have written. I have asked Mr. Smith to drop you a line to show how the matter struck him. With many regrets at the necessity to trouble you, I remain sincerely yours,
R. W. GILDER[10]

If this letter sounds hysterical it reflects not Gilder's hysteria but his desire to *limit* a hysteria. The "new significance" to the word "dynamite" was a hysterical significance given the word by news reports of recent events after Gilder's letter of congratulations in December about the success of the dinner scene. Anarchists had attempted to blow up the Tower of London, Westminster Hall, and the House of Commons on January 24, 1884. On February 17, a report came from London that Socialist agitators had stirred up a mob with intent to dynamite the offices of the Prime Minister. The Paris Conference of the Irish Nationalist Party passed a resolution favoring the use of dynamite to attain its ends.

The following report from the New York *Herald*, February 10, 1885, indicates how exaggerated the hysteria became: "Chicago, Ill., Feb. 9. Within the past few days a meeting of dynamite chiefs has been held in this city. The names and the coming and going of the members from abroad were kept secret. . . . Chicago has always been in the van of Irish revolutionary methods in this country and [it is determined] to give to this city and the Northwest a boom in the dynamite direction." Since *The Century* was published in an English edition, Gilder was probably worried more about the reaction in England than in America. There the hysteria was even worse, and could very conceivably have resulted in the seizure of a magazine in which a character in a novel advocated dynamiting the houses of the rich.

The deleted reference must have been taken from that very same dinner scene at the Corey's that Gilder had praised earlier. Although it is impossible to determine exactly where the reference occurred, it was probably in the discussion following Corey's remark that, if he were a poor man, he would break into one of the

Boston houses left idle while their rich owners summered at the shore, "and camp out on the grand piano":

> "Surely, Bromfield," said his wife, "you don't consider what havoc such people would make with the furniture of a nice house."
>
> "That's is true," answered Corey, with meek conviction. "I never thought of that."
>
> "And if you were a poor man with a sick child, I doubt if you'd have so much heart for burglary as you have now," said James Bellingham.
>
> "It's wonderful how patient they are," said Mr. Sewall, the minister. "The spectacle of the hopeless luxury and comfort the hardworking poor man sees around him must be hard to bear at times." . . .
>
> Sewall added, "I suppose he don't always think of it."
>
> "But some day he *will* think about it," said Corey. "In fact, we rather invite him to think about it, in this country." (XXIX, 866–7)

As a piece of social commentary the scene is not, with or without mention of dynamite, very explosive. Still, it marks an advanced social view on Howells' part several years before his masterpiece in this vein, *A Hazard of New Fortunes.* For *The Century,* it marked but another example of interest in social problems, perhaps the other side of the coin to John Hay's *The Breadwinners.* Howells' intent is clear enough: a reference to violence as a means of changing the social order is implicit in Corey's statement, "Some day he *will* think about it." In short, Gilder was willing to allow discussion of social questions in his pages, even discussion in which the concept of revolution is sympathetically offered. What he objected to was specific allusion to a product that had acquired an inflammatory connotation because of recent events. He was certainly prudent in his behavior but not necessarily timid. Rather, the circumstances seem to justify him. Perhaps he assumed that Howells would restore the missing reference when he published the book. The final evidence of the insignificance of the incident is that Howells did not bother to do so.

IV *Two Editors, One Author*

In October, 1885, Howells signed a contract with Harper Brothers that excluded the possibility of his contributing anything to rival magazines. *The Minister's Charge,* contracted for *The Century* before his commitment, was serialized in the magazine without any important incidents. Howells and Gilder remained friends—in the same social and literary circles, with many of the same friends, it was inconceivable that they should not. But that brief period during which Howells had been the chief contributor to Gilder's magazine was not without influence upon both men. Unquestionably, Gilder was the better editor for his experiences with Howells. Howells was a liberalizing influence on any editor because of his demands upon the editor's willingness to trust him and because of the example of his literary theories. Gilder, as we have seen, admired and respected Howells possibly even to the extent of vicarious enjoyment of his successes. Howells demanded and was accorded more artistic freedom in his writings for the magazine than most editors of the time were wont to give—indeed, more than most modern editors give willingly to their contributors. Gilder responded freely, and his happy experiences with Howells' contributions must have reinforced his willingness to trust the good taste and good sense of his other contributors as well.

It is fortunate that an entirely private and confidential summary of Gilder's feelings about Howells—personal and artistic—is extant. Writing on July 6, 1882, to Professor Daniel Coit Gilman, president of the Johns Hopkins University, in hopes of getting a chair of literature for Howells, Gilder hid nothing of his admiration for Howells, while showing that he was aware of his limitations. After pointing out that Howells, though without a college education, had both "a general knowledge of all English literature and . . . a special and accurate acquaintance with the best modern English writing and of some of the Continental influences which effect it, such as the modern French and Russian writers," Gilder called Howells "a master of the literary art." His evaluation thereafter is both balanced and appreciative: "Having mastered an accurate method, he has in [*A Modern Instance*] brought it to bear upon the most serious concerns. It has seemed to me that much of his earlier writing was rather photographic than imaginative, and that he was inclined to make an effect by minute and clever studies of things so mean as to have been hitherto overlooked. . . . In 'A Modern Instance,' however, the substance is as good as the form. Here is a sincerity, a conviction, an insight which lift the work up into a high artistic plane."

Gilder's most serious criticism of Howells as an editor was that he was likely to be "over sanguine about certain 'rising' young men," but he had to qualify that comment with the observation that "I have in the past at least been so guilty in this respect that I ought not to throw stones." [11] In short, Gilder admired Howells almost without reservation in three areas: as a novelist, personally (even, as I have pointed out, possibly to the extent of vicariously enjoying some of Howells' artistic successes), and in terms of Howells' critical theories.

In the years following their close collaboration, Gilder's admiration naturally became somewhat attenuated; but it never disappeared. More rigid than Howells about the necessity for moral purpose in literature, Gilder in time began to disagree with some of Howells' ideas about the realistic movement in literature. But his admiration for Howells personally and artistically never faltered. To the end of his life, he believed that Howells was one of the greatest contemporary American writers.

As for Gilder's influence on Howells and Howells' opinion of the one American editor with whom he worked successfully as an author for a considerable time, the evidence is ambiguous. Surely those five years of continually successful creative work ought to have taught Howells that it was possible for him to work purposefully without an editorial connection—but he did not choose to do so. Probably Howells *needed* to be both novelist and critic, and there was no "Editor's Easy Chair" or "Editor's Study" available for him in *The Century*. Although Gilder was undoubtedly the most liberal editor with whom Howells was ever connected, Howells needed even more freedom—the freedom to write for his *own* magazine. And he needed a regular outlet for his critical ideas as well. Furthermore, the evidence of his many connections with magazines suggests that perhaps he needed simply the economic security of a steady editorial position, which, of course, Gilder could not give him.

Howells deferred to Gilder's capacity for the criticism of poetry and noted on several occasions his agreement with Gilder's critical observations on prose as well. But his critical ideas were all formulated, or at least germinated, before his contacts with Gilder; and

Gilder could not have influenced him in that area. Rather, Gilder's more timid seconding voice in the problem of realism in fiction probably embarrassed Howells more than it pleased him.

They both believed in the obligation of the magazine editor to censor anything that would bring the blush of shame to an American girl, but each had enough practical reason to arrive at that conclusion without help from the other. The same holds true for most of the opinions of either man about anything having to do with the position of the magazine in American life. Each was an editor; each was fully acquainted with the conditions that prevailed; each arrived at the inescapable conclusions; and there can be no question of influence.

Formed in the same crucible of the inexorable demands of magazine publishing, neither was able to break away entirely from the necessity of producing entertainment for a million readers. Gilder felt editorial pressure somewhat more than did Howells and is, consequently, nearly forgotten today. Howells, who as a critic recommended literature which he could not accept for the magazines he edited, is studied as a force in literature; and he was so, we might almost say, in spite of his connections with the magazines of his day. Howells could not be in contention with Gilder as he was with Holland; Gilder had no need to liberalize Howells as he did Holland; neither man felt an obligation to recognize the genius in the other as both did for Mark Twain. In short, neither man really needed the other, except for that brief but fruitful period between 1881 and 1885. Although their courses in life ran almost exactly parallel, their lives were bridged only briefly. In a way, that fact is the measure of both men: Howells, who became the recognized literary leader of his age, sponsored young writers from Stephen Crane to Robert Frost; but he could find no quarrel with Gilder. Gilder has been identified with the "genteel tradition" by most modern literary historians, but he agreed on nearly all points with Howells. Perhaps this paradox reflects a misapprehension about both men; certainly, it suggests that Gilder's position was far more liberal than has generally been recognized.

But the relationship between the two was that of editors, by and large, in agreement. No one has accused Gilder of bowdlerizing Howells, or, indeed, of exercising anything but an editorial influence which was not at all unfamiliar to Howells. The story of Gilder's relationship with Howells reveals Gilder's extreme competence as an editor, but tells little of his liberalism or of his capacity to see beyond his own age; for Howells, though a fine writer, was unquestionably of his own age. To observe Gilder's capabilities to edit a writer outside the limitations of the "genteel tradition," we must turn our attention now to the rebel *par excellence* of the nineteenth century—Mark Twain.

CHAPTER 7

Mark Twain

I *Contention and Friendship*

IF EVER two men gave each other reasons for a feud instead of a friendship, Samuel Langhorne Clemens and Richard Watson Gilder did. The trouble all started when, in September, 1884, Clemens overheard Gilder discussing with a third person the great good fortune of the Century Company in having nearly acquired the signature of Ulysses S. Grant on a contract for the publication of his memoirs. Now, Gilder was associated with Century Company, and he knew that Clemens was associated with Charles L. Webster and Company, but . . . Gilder *said* that he considered the information private and confidential, while Twain *said*—well, as a matter of fact, he had nothing to say on this aspect of the disagreement; but he said plenty about what followed.

Twain rushed to Grant while Grant was looking over a rough draft of the Century Company's contract, offered him far more liberal terms, and got him to agree to a contract with Charles L. Webster and Company on the spot. If Twain was reticent about how he got his information in the first place, he certainly was not about how and why he got Grant to sign the contract so quickly and easily. Century Company, according to Twain, was either guilty of gross stupidity or positively wanted to cheat Grant out of his due royalties by offering him only ten per cent of the gross. Twain *knew*, he said, that Grant's memoirs should sell one hundred thousand copies, and a royalty of only ten per cent on a sale that large would, indeed, be absurdly small. Century Company's side of the story was that Grant had objected to the idea of paying "a scalawag canvasser $6 for selling a $12 book"; and, with the possibility of subscription sales ruled out (upon which, of course, Twain's estimates were entirely based), Century Company made its plans on properly conservative estimates. Had Grant's objection to subscription selling been removed, the company could have met and bettered Twain's offer; but Century Company was unaware until too late that it was contending with another publishing house.[1]

Everyone knows the sequel: Twain handed Grant's widow the largest royalty check ever paid at that time, and Grant's *Memoirs* kept afloat a series of wild-eyed enterprises like the Paige Typesetting machine. Meanwhile, we can imagine the teeth-gnashing anger that Gilder must have felt at the lost plum, and especially at his part in the losing of it. But he never made his annoyance public, and, anyway, no one could stay angry with Mark Twain for very long. A few months after the incident Gilder was chaffing Twain about his success as a "historian" in "The Private History of a Campaign that Failed":

> It is rumored in New York that you are going to conduct the "Editor's Historical Record" [for *Harper's Magazine*]. This will complete the quartette, Curtis, Howells, Clemens, and Warner. Now if they could get Lord Tennyson to run the advertising department, they need have no fear of Lippincott's Monthly or the Andover Review.
>
> You may think this letter jocose, but it is as solemn and authentic as your War paper. (GL, Oct. 14, 1885)

Indeed, the friendship of Gilder and Twain, though begun inauspiciously, became continuously warmer through Gilder's lifetime. Gilder apparently had a hand in Twain's political evolution —from a Republican through a brief period as a "mugwump" to a voting Democrat. They congratulated each other on their various literary successes; and Twain, as he did with Howells and Twitchell, delighted in testing Gilder's tolerance with slightly obscene allusions and metaphors. To a request by Gilder for an informal talk before a group of journalists, Twain replied, "I can't though I love you just the same. . . . This stud can't abide to stand any more this season" (GP, n.d.). Another letter includes an elaborate scatological pun on the words "Republican statesmanship" (GP, Jan. 6, 1899).

As both men grew older, their friendship became more intense. Gilder was one of many speakers at Twain's seventieth-birthday dinner; but, much more significant than that, he was present at his seventy-first birthday when no one was present "beyond some intimate friends—the Gilders." [2] This new intimacy was reflected in several incidents in which Gilder performed important and very personal services for his friend. In the summer of 1903, for example, Twain's daughter Clara, under severe emotional stress because of her mother's illness, hired an agent and set off on a singing tour through New England on her own. Twain wrote Gilder to collar the "beautiful but tough" Clara and to keep her safe at the Gilder's summer place in Tyringham, Massachusetts (GP, Aug. 1, 1903). Gilder did so, playing the adopted uncle to the distressed girl so well that she "seemed to come into a condition of joyousness which was quite delightful to behold"(GL, Aug. 4, 1903).

When Twain's wife died in 1904, Twain cabled Gilder from Italy, "WE WANT YOUR COTTAGE NEXT YOUR HOUSE FOR THE SUMMER TILL END JUNE," following the cable with a letter asking Gilder to make the necessary arrangements (GP, June 7 [1904]). It was a sad summer for the Clemenses. Gilder described "Mark Twain's sad family next door" as "most grim and unhappy," with Mark especially "full of life and abounding in scorn of a mismanaged universe. Imagine Rabelais and Voltaire rolled into one, discoursing, in the lantern light mixed with moonbeams, of a fiendish and ingenious providence" (LRWG, 362). To make matters worse, a series of accidents and periods of sickness further embittered Twain during the summer. But the beauties of the Berkshires helped ease Twain's mind through a difficult period; and, when the summer ended, he was ready to return to work. He moved back to New York in the fall of 1904, choosing a house at 21 Fifth Avenue, just around the corner from the Gilders' place at 13 East Eighth Street.

Just what position Gilder held in Mark Twain's esteem is an unanswerable question. The documentary evidence of their personal relationship is limited and tends chiefly to relate to their friendship during its least close period between 1880 and 1900. It is very likely that from 1903 to Gilder's death in 1909 the two were very close. Twain seems to have relied more on Gilder than on Howells in the "great Gorky scandal" of 1906. Gilder's daughter, Rosamond, remembers being held in awe by Twain's white hair, mustache, and gruff manner during Twain's many visits to her father's house after 1900.[3] Probably the fact that relatively few documents have survived concerning their friendship during this period may be explained by their very closeness. Twain had no need to write Gilder, and vice versa, if they were seeing each other as often as they seem to have done.

All in all, Gilder was probably second to Howells as a "literary man" in Twain's esteem but less important than the Reverend Joe Twitchell as a personal friend. Still, there can be no doubt that, especially during his last years, Twain came more and more to depend upon Gilder in times of crisis; and, in a sense, Gilder supplanted both Twitchell and Howells during those years.

II *The "Ordeal" of Huck Finn*

But, although their friendship is interesting in itself and casts some light on Twain's respect for "literary men," a predilection that has caused much critical commentary during the past forty years, it is not nearly so significant as their editorial relationship. That relationship represents an important skirmish in the critical war initiated by Van Wyck Brooks with the publication of *The Ordeal of Mark Twain* in 1920. Gilder has been accused, along with Olivia Clemens, Howells, and even Twain himself, of emasculating Twain's work to make it fit more neatly into the "genteel tradition," thereby destroying his strength as a writer. No consideration of Gilder as a force in American literature could, therefore, be complete without an analysis of his editorial demands upon the many contributions Twain made to *The Century*. Here is no situation of like minds striving for like artistic ends, as was the case with Gilder's relationship with Howells. Here, instead, is the most western of writers encountering the most eastern of editors. Gilder had had difficulty comprehending the western problems broached by such talented writers as Eggleston and Garland, but what difficulties must he have had with a western writer of genius?

Many of Twain's short stories first appeared in *The Century*, along with selections from two of his most important novels, *Adventures of Huckleberry Finn* and *A Connecticut Yankee in King Arthur's Court*, plus the complete serialization of a third novel, *Pudd'nhead Wilson*. It is a simple matter to compare the two forms of publication for these works and to conclude from such a comparison the nature and the extent of Gilder's influence upon Twain.

Twain's short fiction, except for insignificant typographical variants, is identical in *The Century* and in later collections. There is no record of editing difficulties about any of Twain's short stories, and for good reason: Twain was a much more skillful writer than most of the contributors to *The Century*. His stories were well constructed, they did not degenerate into polemics as Cable's sometimes did, and his command of dialect was equal to that of any writer of the South or West. These were the three points upon which Gilder had insisted most strongly with his other writers, and as long as Twain's judgment could be trusted in regard to construction, moralizing, and dialect, he was likely to avoid conflict with his editor.

But more important, Twain was only too aware of the restrictions on periodical publications. He had been a newspaperman, had associated with such editors as Gilder and Howells, and was aware of their feelings about what was proper for a magazine and what was suitable for a book. Unlike many of the writers of his day, he was also capable of producing both varieties of fiction. His short works were intended for a magazine audience. Only when he essayed book-length themes did he consciously attempt situations, characters, and language that might prove unacceptable to an audience that "paid in advance."

Garland could never extend his savage indignation, so striking in some of his short stories, to book length; Eggleston's novels were all more or less innocuous; Twain wrote the first literary masterpiece in the American vernacular, *Huckleberry Finn*. Gilder, though he had no opportunity to serialize the novel, published three excerpts from it in *The Century* between December, 1884, and February, 1885. All three of the excerpts were edited, the third one considerably, for publication in the magazine.[4]

The important point is that *The Century's Huckleberry Finn* was *not* a serialization of the novel. In all the years of Gilder's editorship, this instance was one of only two in which excerpts from a novel were published in the magazine, instead of a complete serialization.[5] The cases are very different. An editor's emendations in a serialized novel are imposed upon the writer in terms of the value of the total work; they represent the imposition of his will over that of the writer. In the case of excerpts from a novel, the magazine editor's intentions may be much more humble; instead of making value judgments on the work he is editing by cutting and changing the text. His emendations may very well be imposed by the physical restrictions of his format—the need for space, for example, or the need to reduce the structure of the larger creation (the novel) to a coherent form in its magazine appearance (an episode). Gilder's intent, as we shall see, was to publish three self-contained episodes which were never intended to, indeed, could not, reveal the scope and depth of the novel. To that end, his revisions and deletions, we might expect, were primarily intended to fit the episodes into the space available in the magazine, and to preserve the continuity of each selection, independent of the purpose of the whole novel. That these were indeed Gilder's primary concerns in the editing of the excerpts may be seen very clearly from the fact that all but four variants in *The Century* text occur in the third episode, the most loosely organized of the three.

A second consideration springs immediately from the first. When editing a novel for serial publication, the editor works from a manuscript which may or may not be in a polished, final form. In the case of *The Century* excerpts from *Huckleberry Finn,* Gilder was working from the manuscript of a novel already in print! Indeed, as we have noted, the English edition of the novel was published and on sale several months before the final excerpt appeared in *The Century.* It is even possible, since there is no evidence either for or against it, that Gilder worked from a galley proof of the novel. Such an arrangement served as a constant reminder to the editor, if he needed one, that whatever was published in the magazine would have no influence on the text of the book. We can hardly think of a better way to remind an editor of the ephemeral nature of magazine publishing, but the lesson may be forgotten by critics eager to collate the texts.[6]

Turning to the three excerpts, we find a striking difference between the editing of the first two and the third. Fifty-seven of fifty-eight deletions occur in the third excerpt, but a comparison of the three shows clearly why Gilder cut so much from the final episode when he did almost no cutting from the first two. The second excerpt, published in January, 1885, under the title, "Jim's Investments and King Sollermun," need detain us only briefly. Only two

and a half pages long and located at the very end of the main
body of the magazine, it is obviously a filler item. There are no
deletions in the text published in *The Century*, and there is only
one variant. In the book text, Jim's joke about being rich because
he owns himself and is worth eight hundred dollars is followed by
the comment, "I wisht I had de money, I wouldn' want no mo'."
In *The Century* this comment is replaced by, "But livestock's too
resky, Huck;—I wisht I had de eight hund'd dollars en somebody
else had de nigger." This revision appears possibly to be by
Twain's hand, and it has significance in two minor areas. It is the
only evidence that Twain read the proofs of any of the extracts
that appeared in *The Century*, and it suggests his careless attitude
toward *The Century* selections from his novel, since, if the change
is actually his own, he did not choose to incorporate an obvious
improvement into any edition of the book.

"An Adventure of Huckleberry Finn: with an Account of the
Famous Grangerford-Shepherdson Feud" perfectly describes the
first excerpt, published in December, 1884. It begins with two
introductory paragraphs describing the lazy life aboard the raft,
taken from the chapter following the feud episode, Chapter XIX.
Then follows the paragraphs ending Chapter XVI, omitting the
reference to the snakeskin, which was irrelevant to *The Century*
selection. Chapters XVII and XVIII conclude the excerpt with
only one deletion and one change. The change: in the first line of
Chapter XVII, "In about half a minute" in *The Century* text is
substituted for "In about a minute" in the book text—probably
nothing more than a proofreader's error.

The deletion—the delightful "Ode to Stephen Dowling Bots,
Dec'd," and the few lines introducing it—is one of the best examples of deletion for spatial reasons only. This selection, like both
the others, ends at the bottom of a page in *The Century*, and quite
obviously Gilder felt that these thirty lines could most easily be
spared from *The Century* excerpt to fit the selection into the available space. Everything else in the two chapters has either the dramatic unity of the Grangerford-Shepherdson feud or the single
point of view of Huck's innocent-eye observations of the Granger-
ford household to recommend it. The verses are offered by Twain
as a kind of documentary evidence of Huck's observations on Em-
meline.

In view of the criticisms of Gilder's deletions in the third excerpt, it is interesting to note what was left in the second one. The Grangerford-Shepherdson feud is certainly not namby-pamby literature, and Gilder did not shrink from allowing his readers to encounter some sharp satire on customs and religion in this episode. There is Huck's comment on *Pilgrim's Progress*, that it is a book about "a man that left his family it didn't say why." There is the comparison between hogs and men on churchgoing: "If you notice, most folks don't go to church only when they've got to; but a hog is different." [7] Some of the images of the feud are far from bloodless. When Buck and his brother, dying, are carried down the river while the Shepherdsons run "along the bank shooting at them and singing out 'kill them kill them!'," it may well have made some others besides Huck sick. Such statements are certainly no less powerful than many of the deleted passages of the third excerpt.

But these two excerpts are largely forgotten in the hue and cry over Gilder's supposed bowdlerization of *Huckleberry Finn* in the third selection, "Royalty on the Mississippi: as Chronicled by Huckleberry Finn," published in February, 1885. Any defense of (or attack upon) Gilder as an editor necessarily requires a more detailed examination of this one excerpt than I have done with any other contribution edited by Gilder. Essentially, Gilder's liberalism as an editor must stand or fall on his treatment of this one selection. All of the evidence to the contrary notwithstanding, if Gilder can be convicted of bowdlerizing even a section of *Huckleberry Finn* without good reason, it would be silly to pretend that he stands as a liberal apex above all the other editors of his day.

As for the physical considerations, the third excerpt deals with two incidents of the novel centering on the characters of the Duke of Bilgewater and the Dauphin: the exhibition of the Royal Nonesuch and the fleecing of the Wilks family. In *The Century* the selection runs for twenty-four pages, or about twenty-four thousand words. It is culled from Chapters XIX through XXVIII of the novel, or nearly thirty-three thousand words. More than one-fourth of the material was, therefore, omitted. There are fifty-eight omissions (plus two revisions), ranging in length from a single word to three thousand six hundred words.

All of the variants could be included within three classes, based on what seems evidently to have been Gilder's purpose in editing the selection. First, deletions of language which Gilder could have thought unsuitable for publication in *The Century*. Second, deletions of sentiments, descriptions, or situations for the same reasons. Third, deletions intended to improve the narrative by eliminating material that does not advance the main action of the selection, interferes with the continuity, or is unnecessarily repetitive, overstated, or conclusive.

But, says the critic, if any deletions actually fit into classes one or two, the game is up; for that would certainly be evidence of bowdlerization. But that is not quite true, because underlying all three of these reasons for deletions and more important than any of them is Gilder's primary purpose for all of the deletions in the selection—the saving of space. Surely that was the most important consideration for an editor faced with more than thirty pages of text to be crammed into twenty-four magazine pages. Every deletion Gilder made for whichever of the three reasons listed above was *required* of him in the sense that, if one passage were not taken out, another, equally long, would have to be. It was never a question of "cut it or leave it?" Rather it was, "cut here or cut there?" If cut he must, it is only reasonable that he do some cutting of elements that could provoke angry letters to the editor.

No one could argue that Gilder did not intend to edit from the manuscript words and phrases which he felt might be objectionable to his readers. Gilder himself, when he asked Twain for permission to publish the excerpts, made that fact very clear: "A good deal would have to be omitted on acct [*sic*] of space—and in omitting we might also have a regard for our audience. But I have a pretty 'robustuous taste' (for a pharisaical dude) and wouldn't mutilate your book you may be sure." [8]

Deletions which fall into class one, unsuitable language, include seven excisions and one substitution for a total of twenty-five words. These examples prove that Gilder preferred, when he had the choice, not to print such mild profanity as "dern your skin" and "by jings," and earthy words like "sweat," "rot," and "hogwash." Considering that these deletions were only for the excerpt and not for the book, the loss to American literature is small.

It is surprising to note how few deletions fall into the second class, "ungenteel" sentiments, situations, and descriptions. Only four were made clearly for that reason and eleven others less certainly so. Of the four deletions unquestionably exhibiting the suppression of what Gilder considered an impropriety, only one is really important, and it is the single example of bad editing on Gilder's part. That excision is the line at the bottom of the poster advertising the Royal Nonesuch and the Duke's comment upon it: "Then at the bottom was the biggest line of all which said: LADIES AND CHILDREN NOT ADMITTED/'There,' says he, 'if that line don't fetch them, I don't know Arkansaw!' " Without the line and the Duke's comment, the joke is lost; the reason for the increased attendance at the three performances of the Royal Nonesuch is no longer evident. And yet, what was Gilder to do? The point of the incident is little more than a dirty joke.[9] The phallic nature of the King's portrayal is hardly less obvious in *The Century* than it is in the book. Gilder would have had to leave out the entire section about the Duke and the King had he not decided to risk printing a truncated form of this incident. Hazy as it is in *The Century*, the impression of an obscene performance remains, in spite of this deletion and that of the word "naked" from the description of the King's costume in the following paragraph.

The other deletions in this class are much less damaging to the total effect of the selection. The reference to the pretty girls who kissed the King at the revival meeting doubtless would have shocked some of *The Century's* readers. If it is missed, it is not at the expense of *The Century* text's total exposure of the King's character. The same could be said of the King's blasphemous remark about trusting to Providence for his ill-gotten gains. Huck's reference to hiding under the bed "when you are up to anything private" has a fainter and more subtle flavor of the forbidden. Perhaps Gilder deserves more credit for catching the innuendo than blame for suppressing it in his magazine.

It is impossible to say what exactly was in Gilder's mind as he made the eleven deletions which seem to fit into both groups two and three. The description of the Arkansas town is cut by two deletions, both rather lengthy. The first is an unlovely picture of houses and gardens; the second describes the inhabitants, their tobacco-chewing habits, and their ill-treatment of dogs. Neither is important to the excerpt as it appears in *The Century*, and elsewhere Gilder deleted setting and description that is not at all objectionable (the description of the print shop where the Duke printed his handbills, for example). Still, both these descriptions are so sordidly realistic that Gilder was doubtless not unhappy to exclude them from *The Century*.

The other deletions partake as much of unnecessary overstatement of facts already in evidence as they do of the 1885 idea of obscenity. The appearance of the King's costume as the Royal Nonesuch may be discerned in *The Century* without Huck's comment: "but never mind the rest of his outfit; it was just wild, but it was awfully funny." Similarly, the character of the ammunition brought by the third-night audience is apparent in *The Century* without the burlesque comments of Huck about knowing "the signs of a dead cat" and the fact that the audience could turn the missed performance into a picnic since "they brought plenty provisions." The description of Jim in his Arab costume is adequately horrendous without Huck's final line, "Why, he didn't only look like he was dead, he looked considerably more than that." In fact, the statement, amusing as it is, is uncalled for; for nothing in the more direct description preceding it leads to it as a conclusion. Jim is described as being more dangerous than dead.

Deletions of the same type in the Wilks family episode also seem to have been made more on esthetic grounds than on moral ones. Huck's comment, "and both of them took on about that dead tanner like they'd lost the twelve disciples. Well, if ever I struck anything like it, I'm a nigger," is pretty much a duplication of what precedes it; and it is followed by the much more striking comment, which was kept in *The Century* text, "It was enough to make a body ashamed of the human race." Three references excised from this section describing the body and the coffin of Peter Wilks are not any more revolting than the references to death and corpses left in *The Century* version of the Grangerford-Shepherdson feud, and the account of the nose-blowing at Peter Wilks' funeral, deleted by Gilder, is comparable to the observation on hogs and churches left in the earlier episode. Without specific evidence to the contrary, these ought to be considered deletions for tightening of the action, not evidence of Gilder's lack of "robustuous taste."

The thirty-five remaining deletions, ranging in length from a single word, a redundant "together," to thirty-six hundred words, are remarkable testimony to how good an editor Gilder was. Most of them represent simply the removal of extraneous verbiage, but

some are interesting evidences of what Gilder intended the excerpt to represent, and others reveal remarkable examples of Gilder's critical judgment. Gilder invariably deleted passages in
which Twain's passion for burlesque or for sentimentalism got the
better of his critical sense. Thus the text in *The Century* does not
include the curious rendition of Hamlet's soliloquy or Huck's epic
simile on "harrow" mumps. Burlesque might add to the flavor of
the novel, but it was out of place in the self-contained episode
published in *The Century,* in which the Duke and the King are
the central characters. Sentimentality got even shorter shrift
under Gilder's editorial hand: excised from *The Century* text are
Jim's woeful story of his discovery of his daughter's deafness, the
tears dropped into Peter Wilks' coffin, and the gross emotionalism
of Huck's final interview with Mary Jane Wilks. They are not
missed.

We should not claim too much for Gilder in his cancelling of
these passages. His primary purpose was the saving of space and
the reduction of the picaresque narrative to an integrated episode.
These purposes are more clearly visible in the deletions of references to material not included within this episode. A reference to
"Buck's folks," the Grangerfords, is expunged, along with a reference to Huck's Pap. More important, a rather long passage (176
words) pertaining to the growth of mutual respect between Huck
and Jim was deleted by Gilder, since that theme of the novel had
no place in *The Century* excerpt.

In sum, we could wish that Twain had had time to look over the
emendations made by Gilder and to consider the possibility of
including some of them in a later edition of the book. Doubtless
he would have done so if *The Century* version had been a serialization of the novel, but that, emphatically, was not the case. Publishing excerpts from a novel already at the press constituted a
unique use of *The Century's* great circulation, then over two hundred thousand. Besides paying Twain $1300 for the three selec-
tions, Gilder was doing his part to publicize the novel. The final
deletion of the third episode, a reference to the appearance of the
real heirs of Peter Wilks, serves to conceal the resolution of the
Wilks episode; and in no serial of *The Century* is the reader left
quite so high and dry as he is at the end of this excerpt. In this
case, however, the reader is not to await the next issue; he must
instead buy the book. During the months the excerpts were ap-

pearing in *The Century,* Twain was busy reading parts of the novel in his lecture series for the same purpose—to stimulate interest in the novel.[10] He was aware that Gilder was doing him an extraordinary favor by publishing parts of the novel, but was also paying him well for the privilege. Under the circumstances, we are rather struck by the fact that there are not *more* deletions. Gilder certainly had nothing to gain by choosing the Royal Nonesuch episode for his excerpt instead of, for example, the final chapters of the novel about the freeing of Jim. His choice of the much more potentially dangerous Duke and King chapters over the innocuous Tom Sawyer sections shows not only courage but also critical acumen.

Critical insight and courage are also reflected in *The Century's* review of *Huckleberry Finn.* Gilder commissioned Thomas Sargent Perry to write the review shortly after the American edition of the novel appeared. He was the only editor of a major American periodical to give it that attention.[11] Moreover, the review was both commendatory and intelligent. Perry skillfully recognized the virtues of the novel in comparison with *Tom Sawyer*—the continuity provided by the raft journey and the effectiveness of the first-person, innocent-eye narration. His only major criticism— one that is repeated today—is that "where the evident truthfulness of the narrative . . . is lacking, and its place is taken by ingenious invention, the book suffers," as in the artificial rescue of Jim by Huck and Tom Sawyer at the close of the novel. Perry also praised especially the account of the Grangerford-Shepherdson feud in terms reflecting Gilder's opinion of the role of didacticism in art:

> The account of the feud between the Shepherdsons and the Grangerfords . . . is described only as it would appear to a semi-civilized boy of fourteen, without the slightest condemnation or surprise,—either of which would be bad art,—and yet nothing more vivid can be imagined. That is the way that a story is best told, by telling it, and letting it go to the reader unaccompanied by sign-posts or directions how he shall understand it and profit by it. Life teaches its lessons by implication, not by didactic preaching; and literature is at its best when it is an imitation of life and not an excuse for instruction.[12]

III *Aftermath*

Among those who were satisfied with Gilder's handling of the publication of the three excerpts from *Huckleberry Finn* was Twain himself. When in 1889, he was about to publish *A Connecticut Yankee in King Arthur's Court,* he went to Gilder again for the same arrangement: to publish a single excerpt from the novel just before the book was issued. Except that the selection is somewhat shorter, *The Century* episode from *A Connecticut Yankee* (XXXIX, 74–83) is very similar to *The Century's* third excerpt from *Huckleberry Finn.* The earlier excerpt centered on the picaresque characters of the Duke and the King; the later one concentrates on the anachronism of nineteenth-century technology in a medieval setting. For the *Connecticut Yankee* excerpt, however, Gilder was forced to interpolate short summaries of the intervening action, since the episodes chosen were more widely scattered and less unified than had been the case with the third *Huckleberry Finn* selection. The most important difference between the two publications stems from the fact that Gilder apparently had an early form of the manuscript from which he drew his text and, unlike the two texts of *Huckleberry Finn, The Century* text of *A Connecticut Yankee* is, on several points, closer to Twain's original intentions than the book text. In fact, the text as given in *The Century* includes several phrases and descriptions that were edited out of the book text because they were too "ungenteel!"

The selection opens with the introductory paragraph of "The Stranger's History" from the first chapter. In this paragraph two variants occur which are unquestionably closer to the original manuscript than are the equivalent passages in the book text. In *The Century* the Colt arms factory is mentioned by name, while in the book text it is referred to as "the great arms factory." The last sentence in the first paragraph in *The Century* text is, "Well, a man like that is a man that has got plenty of sand." The passage appears in less colloquial dress in the book text: "Well, a man like that is a man that is full of fight." The expression "to have sand" is typically western American in origin and was considered a vulgar colloquial form of "to be brave," or, as in the revised version of Twain's phrase, to be "full of fight." [13] What appeared in *The Cen-*

tury is obviously Twain's original phrase, which was later revised in favor of a phrase less colloquial but, alas, more of a cliché.

After a summary of the action occurring in Chapters II through VI, Gilder printed Chapter VII in full, describing the Yankee's dissatisfaction with life in a medieval castle, his comments on chromos and art, and the blowing up of Merlin's tower. There are seven variants in *The Century* form of the chapter, three of which are insignificant. Of the remaining four, two are either omissions from *The Century* text or additions to the book text: one is a changed form in which the text in *The Century* almost surely represents the original; and the last is, *mirabile dictu,* a deletion in the book text. In each case, the text in *The Century* is superior and is, again, nearer Twain's original manuscript than is the equivalent in the published text.

The two "omissions" are problematical. For the first one, the statement "Raphael was a bird" is not present in *The Century* text of Hank Morgan's railing upon the lack of realism in medieval tapestries. It is impossible to tell whether Gilder deleted it or if Twain added it for the book text. Since such intentionally shocking judgments are so common in Twain's writings, and were sometimes deleted by Gilder in the third *Huckleberry Finn* episode, it is quite possible that its absence is a result of Gilder's blue pencil. But that is only a speculation, and it seems far more likely that the statement was added later. In any case, the statement is not needed to support Hank Morgan's only too clear opinion about Raphael's art.

The second "omission" occurs after Hank advises Merlin to "take boarders" in his new tower, built after the old one has been blown up. Missing from the text in *The Century* is Hank's ironic comment: "And as for being grateful, he never even said thank you." If it is indeed an excision by Gilder, we would have great difficulty deducing a reason for his cutting it. Lacking evidence to the contrary, it seems most likely that this statement also was added by Twain to the book text.

After the explosion of Merlin's tower, the Yankee noted that "it rained mortar and masonry the rest of the week." In the text in *The Century* he qualified that statement by adding, "This was the report; but I reckon they added on a couple of days." In the book text, the last sentence reads instead: "This was the report; but probably the facts would have modified it." Like the variant about "having sand," this change suggests that the text in *The Century* is closer to Twain's original manuscript than is the book text. *The Century* statement is more hyperbolic, and therefore more western, than the more subtle irony in the book text.

The fourth variant in this chapter presents the most striking example of Gilder's comparative tolerance for the extravagance of Twain's writing. Hank reports in both book and magazine that, while he was making the preparations to blow up Merlin's tower, he threw Merlin into "the same cell I had occupied myself." In *The Century* he then adds an observation which he is not allowed to make in the book: "and I didn't thin out the rats any for his accommodation." There can be no doubt why this omission was made in the book text. The readers of *The Century* were subjected to this unpleasant detail of a rat-infested cell, occupied first by the Yankee and later by Merlin; but purchasers of the book were not. If the modern critic wishes to conclude that Gilder bowdlerized Twain in the *Huckleberry Finn* selections, it seems that he must then admit that Twain bowdlerized Gilder in *A Connecticut Yankee!* And the case is clearer here than it is in any of the omissions in the last *Huckleberry Finn* episode; there are no omissions because of lack of space in the publication of a book.

The remainder of the text includes many minor variants, none of which is very important except to show that the editing of the excerpt in *The Century* was superior in most ways to the editing of the book. A few examples illustrate the point: In the Yankee's bout with Sir Sagramour and the other knights, Merlin says in the book text that Hank's magic lasso could only be used eight times; in the text in *The Century* the figure is nine. Indeed, a careful count reveals that there had been *nine* bouts, not eight. And then, when Hank faced the charge of knights with only his revolver, the word "squalid" in the book text is obviously a misprint for the word in *The Century*, "squally": "At such a time it is sound judgment to put on a bold face and play your hand for a hundred times more than it is worth: forty-nine times out of fifty nobody dares to 'call,' and you rake in the chips. But just this once—well, things looked squally." Also, as was the case with the third *Huckleberry Finn* episode, Gilder ended this extract with a pique to the interest of possible purchasers of the book by noting that "Merlin . . . got one more chance at the Yankee—and made exceedingly good use of it, too." Whether considered as editor or publicist,

Gilder justified in these excerpts Twain's friendship with him.

In all points, this excerpt parallels the case of the third excerpt from *Huckleberry Finn*. Gilder presented a self-contained unit of the book which would interest readers of the magazine without hurting the chances of the book. The differences in the editing of this selection and the *Huckleberry Finn* selections result from the fact that Gilder took his text from a manuscript as yet unedited by Twain (and by Stedman and Howells, who aided him in the final editing of the book). Had the same conditions prevailed with the *Huckleberry Finn* publication—had Gilder edited the text uncorrected by Howells and Twain for final publication—we may be sure that there would have been examples there of variants which would prove that Gilder was far from being a "pharisaical dude," as he put it. But that is, of course, pure hypothesis. What we need is a pure example, a case of the serialization of a novel, not the printing of excerpts. For only a collation of the two forms of a serialized novel can solve once and for all the problem of Gilder's editing of Twain. Happily, the example exists.

Pudd'nhead Wilson, the only one of Twain's novels serialized by *The Century* before book publication, is identical, except for typographical variants, in its two forms. Now, in many ways *Pudd'nhead Wilson,* melodramatic as it is, stands today as the most outspoken of Twain's novels on the subject of social problems. The plot depends wholly on the fact of miscegenation and its corruptive effect upon Negroes and whites alike. Bernard DeVoto pointed out that, in this novel, Twain "states and develops a theme completely tabooed in nineteenth-century American literature" (293). In other words, *Pudd'nhead Wilson* seems an unlikely candidate for serialization in a "genteel" magazine like *The Century,* edited by "bowdlerizer" Gilder. Nevertheless, it was the readers of *The Century* who first encountered *all* of the text of this novel of miscegenation. And it was the "bowdlerizing" Gilder who shocked his audience (some one hundred and fifty thousand subscribers in 1894) with Roxy's proud boast that her son was descended from "de highest quality in dis whole town—ole Virginny stock," and the bitter irony of her reminder to him: "Dey ain't another nigger in dis town dat's as high-bawn as you is. . . . Jes you hold yo' head up as high as you want to—you has de right, en dat I kin swah" (XLVII, 550, 551).

Critics who have accused Gilder of emasculating Twain's writing chose to examine only part of their relationship. Viewing the whole, we must conclude that the opposite is true. Gilder displayed remarkable courage in all his dealings with Twain, printing one work that defied a major restriction on American literature and publicizing two other major works. Gilder's relations with Twain could not have been so cordial—indeed, intimate—if he had not had the capacity to recognize and honor Twain's genius—and to extend his own moral courage to the point of acting against the taste of his time. Any one of Mark Twain's publications which appeared in *The Century* could have been passed over in favor of some vapid magazine fiction. Instead, Gilder chose to suffer the criticisms of his readers for publishing works which challenged the moral standards of his day. His reward was to be misunderstood by two ages: damned in his own day for immorality and bad literary judgment, he has been damned in our day for prudery and bad literary judgment.

CHAPTER *8*

Critic, Editor, Man of Letters

GILDER'S age was one of transition. We have seen examples of his part in the making of many changes in American literature: his espousal of the new voice in American poetry contributed by Walt Whitman; his assistance in the rebirth of letters in the South and particularly his liberal attitude toward the social problems of the Negro; his deliberate choice of American letters over those of Europe; his accommodation of the new kind of literature being written by Howells and, especially, by Mark Twain. His editorial function included *ex officio* the function of critic, and we have seen by his choice of literature in what directions his critical tastes ran. Actions do speak louder than words; but, having considered his editorial choices and accommodations, his acceptance of responsibility toward the American writer and the American public which he also served—it is time now to consider his more specifically critical statements, his literary theories, his visions of the purpose of literature.

The great bulk of Gilder's critical writing concerns three subjects only, but they are the three which were most in contention during his nearly forty years of literary prominence. First is the role of realism in fiction, the struggle between realism and romanticism as the dominant manner of expression in literature; and, necessarily, there is the concomitant question of good taste in the expression of sexual themes in literature. Second is the position of the magazine as a literary force, the obligation of the magazine to the American public and to the writers whom it supports and by whom it is supported. Third is a problem to which Gilder devoted more of his energy than to either of the others: the question of international copyright. His positions on these three points not only suggest a good deal about his importance as an editor but also illustrate the state of American literature at the end of the nineteenth century.

[140]

I *The* "Real *Real in Literature*"

One might expect that Gilder would have been totally opposed to the concept of realism in literature. After all, he was committed to the principle of idealism—in poetry particularly, but by extension in fiction as well. But realism and idealism in literature are not mutually exclusive; the opposite of realistic fiction is *romantic* fiction, not idealism. In fiction, idealism is not necessarily romanticism but an insistence upon the recognition of some higher values, on motivation beyond self-interest, for example, or, in Gilder's words, the importance of "those actual experiences of the heart, those natural passions and delights which have created in man the 'romantic spirit'; those experiences of the soul which have created in him 'the religious spirit,' and which are facts of existence certainly no less important than any others." [1]

Gilder's position in the conflict between realism and romanticism was like his stance in many other controversies—that of the conciliatory man of common sense. He believed that each of the opposing parties overstated his case since "there are few realists who have no ideality, and few idealists, few romanticists, who do not make use of the real. . . . The fact is that all art is a selection. There is no *real* real in literature" (*NPR*, 1). This argument, with which few critics would disagree, is bolstered by Gilder's frank belief that the realists were doing "a great and needed work, both by example and precept," when they opposed the sentimental and absurd in romantic fiction. But he found that the realists themselves were wrong when they senselessly ignored the beautiful and "delighted in the disgusting." The answer to the problem, then, was not to return to the sentimental but to improve the new form: "The more reality the better! But let it be reality all the way through; reality of the spirit as well as of the flesh; not grovelling reality; not a reality microscopic, or photographic, or self-conscious, or superficial: nor a reality that sees ugliness but is blind to beauty! not a reality which sees the little yet neither sees nor feels the great" (*NPR*, 5–6).

Obviously, Gilder is paralleling Howells' belief that American writers ought to "concern themselves with the more smiling aspects of life, which are the more American." [2] But their positions are quite different, chiefly because of their different emphases.

Howells emphasized the need for more realism; for him, the American writer's concern with the "smiling aspects of life" was simply a fact of American reality. Gilder, on the other hand, feared the course realism would take; if it concerned itself less with the smiling aspects than with man's baser nature, it would become as unreal a view of life as the romantic writers' overemphasis of ideal behavior.

Gilder's belief springs from a misapprehension which is central to his critical thought about realism. He believed that "realism . . . is the state of mind of the nineteenth century" (*NPR*, 4). His chronology is bad because he viewed realism from his own experience and could not or would not see that realism as a state of mind (in the last two decades of the nineteenth century in America) was really a reaction from the prevalent state of mind of the nineteenth century, the romantic and the ideal. This misapprehension tells more about his own ideas about realism than is at first apparent, and the ramifications of it are important. As an editor, Gilder certainly knew that romanticism, sentimentalism, and idealism were far from dead in 1886. Most of the manuscripts submitted to *The Century* were romantic and idealistic. Therefore, his belief that realism "is the state of mind of the nineteenth century" proves that in his opinion the battle had been won, that creative writers of realistic fiction had shown that they were far more capable of producing significant work than the sub-literary writers of romantic fiction.

Having arrived at that position, Gilder found it no great step to the position he finally occupied: realistic writers could profit from taking the best elements from the romantic writers—not sentimentalism, not vagaries of plot, but the recognition of motives beyond those generally ascribed by realistic writers to their characters. "We do not want less realism, but more of it; and better, fuller than we now have! In some of our current realistic work a true method, used awkwardly by men freshly and deeply enamoured therewith, becomes obvious and ineffectual. The result is a straining after novelty; the elevation of the insignificant; in a word, a lack of proportion, a lack of art" (*NPR*, 6).

This position seems to have derived from Howells, but from his example, not his precept. Gilder believed that *The Rise of Silas Lapham* was an example of the realism which he could praise without hesitation. The character of Silas fulfills all his criteria for the ideal realistic character. Howells' delineation of all Silas' faults, yet his insistence upon Silas' nobility of character in accepting ruin rather than to take part in an immoral act, is precisely Gilder's notion of the proper function of realism. Possibly Gilder saw in Silas a prototype of a new realistic hero who succeeded in fusing the best of the real with the ideal.

In Gilder's misappraisal of the element of reaction in the movement for realism in fiction, he doomed himself to inevitable disappointment. There was no possibility of fusing the two movements as he wanted. During his lifetime, realism became more stark; romanticism, less related to human values. Faced with the editorial choice between a realism that ignored nobility of character and a romanticism that ignored human motivation, Gilder came more and more to choose what seemed to him the lesser evil. In the process he acted, upon occasion, like the conservative editor that the modern stereotype suggests he was all the time. When Stephen Crane, the nephew of an old friend from Newark, brought him the manuscript of *Maggie,* Gilder, the editor of a middle-class magazine, sat in judgment, but not as Gilder the critical theorist. The incident, apocryphal as it is, is nevertheless revealing. Gilder, after reading the story, protested that it was "cruel," and gave examples of excessive detail. Crane interrupted, "You mean the story is too honest?" Gilder the editor faded, and Gilder the liberal theorist nodded an unhappy acquiescence.[3]

Maggie is an unfair test of Gilder's editorial courage, for no editor was willing to accept it, and Crane eventually had to publish it privately. But Gilder's evolution as a critical theorist becomes evident if we compare his ideas in 1886, discussed above, with another comment on contemporary literature written just ten years later. The factors are all the same—perfection in literature can be achieved only through a combination of the real and the ideal—but the emphasis has shifted: "'Reality' is a word to conjure with; anyone who raises a 'blue pencil' against reality is in peril of losing his literary standing. The editor is prone to level things down; to object to the novel and original; he may be a Philistine; he may even be touched with hypocrisy. But if there is any greater humbug and hypocrisy than 'realism' can be, I do not know what it is." [4] This is also the editor speaking. Gilder could not very well print the works of Mary Hartwell Catherwood and refuse Crane's *Maggie* without having recourse to some such justification of his actions. When realism became too detailed, too "honest" in revealing the more sordid factors of life—as Gilder thought, disproportionately—it became to his mind a greater hypocrisy than romantic insistence upon ideal values and actions.

During the last decade of his life, Gilder took another step toward the conservative view by introducing a new term to describe what he felt to be a new kind of literature. "The Genial in Literature" is the title of an editorial in *The Century* for April, 1903, in which he attempted once more to bridge the widening gap between realistic and romantic fiction. His choice of terms was unfortunate; the word "genial" does not describe works like Ethel Noyes Wescott's *David Harum* and the novels of Kate Wiggins nearly so well as "inconsequential" does. But his defense of the new term and the fiction it described shows the final degeneration of his critical sense: "In the rush and strain of modern life is the genial especially valued. The romantic has been of late warmly welcomed, by contrast to straining modern conditions, but the genial seems now, in America, to be living up promisingly to [its] claims" (LXV, 959). Critically, it is impossible to defend a champion of escape literature.

What happened to Gilder as a defender of realism ought to be a warning to all critics of all ages. Though he welcomed the rise of realism in 1886, he never understood it. What he thought was a breath of fresh air come to revive a romanticism that had deteriorated into Gothic improbability was actually a whirlwind that had to destroy all the old values before it could build its own. Not comprehending that the productions of a valued friend and respected editor like Howells could really be a reaction against all the romantic tenets, and thus a precursor of an even more explicit realism, Gilder hoped to palliate the differences between two methods or styles that did not seem to him to be mutually exclusive, thereby arriving at something which he hoped would be far better than either. Alas for him, the differences grew larger and more fundamental; and by the end of his career he was forced to choose between the two approaches and styles. From the modern point of view he chose incorrectly, but from his own position as editor-in-chief of one of the most popular magazines in America, there could be no other choice.

II *Sexual Expression*

The problem of realism in literature is inextricably bound with the problem of free discussion. Gilder's basic theory of the proper subjects for literature is one that might be held by any good critic. "It is the essence of literature," he wrote, "that it should be free. It must criticize life without reserve—except such reserve as is expected by the principles of good taste." [5] The difficulty is implicit in the qualifying phrase, for the principles of good taste are constantly changing. Taste, at least for the past century, has been a function of time; today's barbarian is tomorrow's conservative, and yesterday's liberal is today's prude.

By most modern standards, Gilder was an indubitable prude. He declined an article on the career of an artist's model, admittedly well written and interesting, because some of the descriptions of her "attitudinizing" dealt "with matters which are not expected to be in the *Century*" and which, if published there, "would excite some surprise" (GL, Nov. 10, 1894). One of Hogarth's engravings for "The Rake's Progress" was left out of Timothy Cole's "Old Masters" series because of its supposed sensuality; and John Hay was asked to revise parts of *The Breadwinners* to remove evidences of the hero's "rakishness." [6]

Gilder's most explicit statement about good taste and the expression of sexual motifs in literature occurs in a letter to George Silvester Viereck. Writing to a young poet whom he wanted to help, Gilder was as unsparing in his criticisms of Viereck as he was in his revelation of himself. When Viereck quoted parts of the letter in a tributary article to Gilder, he left out sections which reveal his own squeamishness; but the entire letter is germane to this question:

13 East 8th St., N. Y.
June 24, '07.

MY DEAR MR. VIERECK,

The reason I have not before written is that I have felt I had so much to say about your book that I was in the condition of one choked in the utterance. And then has come the further conviction that it would be foolish to say all I had to say. This final conviction is now upon me—and so I shall be brief. You do not need that I should repeat my appreciation of the genuineness of your gift. I have read and re-read the book "Nineveh," and am struck by its qualities of imagination and power of expression shown. There is in the expression an energy, a directness, and force,—a propriety of phrase most satisfying. Only now and then are there touches of foreignness, or of verbal imitation, or wordiness. There are things in this book that give great promise—and there is much of remarkable accomplishment.

Of the things that you know perfectly well repel me I imagine it is hardly worth while, or useful, for me to say anything. You would discount, naturally, anything I might say—and turn for justification to brilliant precedent, and to the praise of bright minds.

Let me nevertheless be true to that which I am sure you do not despise in me and say that one of the pieces, for instance, gives me the feeling of physical repulsion I remember having had when I have seen a man coming out of a house of prostitution.

There are all sorts of ways of dealing in art with the sex phenomena—some entirely legitimate—I don't object to the nude —but to the disgusting —to something that suggests a bad smell, and to a certain self-satisfaction in the parade of the knowledge of vice.

Now neither in life nor in literature can one "eat his cake and have it." One cannot associate on mutually respecting terms with the purest and noblest women and men—and at the same time be suspected of vaunting something repulsive in the mind. I am saying this on general principles and after looking over the whole range of modern literature. If you doubt that I have a pretty strong stomach—see this month's American—and what Whitman says about the way I treated him—author of the unblushing Leaves of Grass.—[sic]

There is a tendency to offset sensuality, of some sort—with Christliness—There is too much of the Katzenjammer about that for my taste, so I don't get as much satisfaction out of that part of the Nineveh book as I ought to.

I have an immense respect for sin, but I cherish no illusions about vice. It is only an evidence of a certain grade in evolution.

The older I grow the more tolerant I find myself with "human frailty," so called; with lack of control; with actions or thoughts showing that humanity in individuals and in the large is simply evolving slowly. I can easily forgive all this—in myself—in others. But I have no illusions about it. On the other hand the older I grow the more do I become a militant purist. For I know, I *know* that pure love is incomparably beyond lust; and I *know* that the only sane aim of life is the noble, the well-nigh unattainable best. And especially do I intensely feel that *noblesse oblige* applies above all to the Poet. You remember what Milton says in that wonderful passage, "I was confirmed in this opinion that he who would not be frustrate of his hope to write well hereafter in laudable things, ought himself to be a true poem—that is a composition and pattern of the best and honourablest things." [7]

Perhaps the nature in contemporary literature, on this side the water, most like Keats in sensitiveness to sensuous beauty was Lafcadio Hearn. It is most interesting, in his life and letters, to watch his development through experience of true love and of fatherhood into absolute responsibility and devotion of character. He lived through illusion into the deepest realities. He now determined that his children should be brought into a knowledge and friendship of the "best and honorablest."

I seem to be pouring on to your head a lot of pent-up thinking and feeling occasioned by various recent circumstances. Wherever it fits—if it fits at all—take it as an evidence of my anxious and great interest in your career. Where it doesn't fit—apply it to some "other fellow who may need it."

I was saved some poetic errors by wise advice in my youth. I had some resentment at the time. Please "resent" as little as you can and believe me

Yours in the love of Beauty, in Art—and most of all in Poetry,

R. W. GILDER [8]

Gilder may have been a prude, but he was no hypocrite. The sentiments expressed in his letter to Viereck were part of his theory of literature and may be found everywhere in his critical writings. "There are many who believe that America has the purest society in the world," he wrote. "Is not this purity worth paying for with a little prudery?" (*NPR*, 8). Gilder's published writings on the subject, in fact, are more conservative than his private statements. He could tell Viereck that he found himself growing more tolerant of human frailty, but he wrote in an article in *The Independent,* December 10, 1896, that he was ever on guard, as an editor, against "salaciousness and gross sensationalism." Because of his influential position, Gilder held a stronger line on moral questions in public than he privately felt was necessary.

His prudishness was much more limited in his personal life, although his personal standards were high. Oscar Wilde disgusted him, and he led an effort to keep Wilde out of the Century Club in 1882. But he consistently enjoyed Mark Twain's often off-color humor, and he participated in the sometimes bawdy fraternity of journalists in the Fellowcraft Club. He would take a drink, but disliked intemperance; cut a friend who was guilty of a marital infidelity, but expressed his appreciation for Brander Matthews' epigram; "Divorce will never be as popular as marriage until there are presents."

Gilder's personal morality and his ideas about morality in literature sprang from two main sources: social Darwinism and idealism. As he grew older, Gilder came more and more to believe in social evolution: "We are always animals evolving into balanced, responsible human beings," he wrote (GL, Oct. 21, 1904). Previously, he believed, morality had been acquired only through repression and control by external forces; Gilder looked forward to the day when man would evolve to the point where his own understanding clearly discriminated between right and wrong. In the meanwhile, he felt it his responsibility as an editor to be a force in moral suasion, if only negatively, by not "preaching letting loose."

The other source of his ideas about morality, his idealism, is closely related to his conception of social evolution. Since man is perfectible, Gilder reasoned, he will someday behave in an ideal manner. Until that day, the responsibility of morally advanced persons was to point the way towards moral perfection. Gilder found it hard to understand "a nature craven enough to be willing to put up with anything but the best, the most noble, the absolutely perfect, the spiritually highest." Those who were content with less were men who might say, "I do not like clean bread and meat; give me swill." Every man has the duty to guard his own soul; and, if he does not follow an absolute moral code, "He cannot escape . . . from injuring other souls, either through occasioning grief, or by contamination" (LRWG, 378).

Such were his ethics; and, to his credit in his position as a leader of public opinion, he tried never to breach them through any straining after popularity, either for himself or for his magazine. Yet within the bounds of these self-imposed ideals, Gilder allowed a good deal of latitude, particularly for the all-too-occasional sparks of genius that he recognized in manuscripts submitted to him. For Mark Twain, he could publish a serial novel dealing with the forbidden subject of miscegenation. For William Dean Howells, he could contract to print a novel that was to deal with divorce and marital unhappiness with only an outline of the plot and the author's reputation to assure him that the result would not be disastrous. Critics have chosen to remember Gilder chiefly for his limitations, when actually his performance as an editor within and beyond those limitations is far more remarkable. A moral man, yes, even a morally circumscribed man, Gilder more often than not transcended his personal moral circumscription to achieve greatness as an editor.

III *The Role of the Magazine*

The problem of realism and freedom of expression in literature may seem, retrospectively, the most important critical problem of Gilder's lifetime; but it caused him less anguish than the problem of the role of the magazine in literature. Gilder was a magazine editor first, a man of letters second. Furthermore, his attachment to *The Century* was almost an identification, reaching back to the founding of the magazine and including the evolution of all of its policies. It is only natural that a good deal of his literary theorizing went into justifying the anomalous position held during his lifetime by powerful magazines like *The Century*. His ideas on the subject were developed early and held consistently through his life. One of his earliest statements on the subject, in a letter to Henry James, is also perhaps his best:

> I think there is a wide distinction between what is magazineable and what is bookable. A man has a right to publish what he chooses in his own book—people seldom buy a book without knowing pretty much what is in it. The writer of a book is responsible to his own conscience and to his taste, and if these are satisfied, no criticism can or should move him. But I think it is different with a magazine. People subscribe for twelve issues in advance . . . on the conviction that their contents will not unduly shock or distress the readers of a magazine which does not intend to be a battle ground of opinion in the sense that certain other publications are. (GP, May 29, 1883)

A few years later he amplified these opinions. "The full list of virile works of fiction published in American magazines during the last fifteen or twenty years would be a long one," he wrote.

But the magazine is only one of many avenues of publication open to the writer. He has also "the privilege . . . to print . . . in the newspapers, and book publication, also, is nearly always possible." In sum, Gilder could not believe "that works of real art, of real power, can be prevented from reaching the public in America. Some periodical, some publisher will send them forth, and the author will reap a generous reward" (*NPR*, 9).

Gilder was not blind to the deficiencies of the American magazine as a market for literature, but he emphasized the obligation of the writer to seek a market beyond the magazines for the unsparing fiction and criticism which the magazines could not print. The greater obligation, he felt, belonged to the writer to market his less commercial productions than to the magazines to change their policies. Nevertheless, he was aware of the dangers implicit in the situation: "A very large proportion of our very best literature has been and will be fostered by the magazines. There is just this danger in the magazine—that its peculiar audience and traditions may unwittingly somewhat cripple the literary criticism of life. This danger may have been exaggerated by certain of our novelists, but it is a point to be considered with regard to the future of American literature." [9]

If these statements sound defensive, the reason should be obvious. Gilder had one of the most responsible and unenviable positions that ever existed in the history of any national literature. As the editorial personification of one of the most influential magazines of the day, Gilder was a ruler of American taste in letters. He ruled, however, not as a monarch but as a representative; he was dependent in his turn upon that manifestation of democracy in the magazine—circulation. Moreover, he was receptive to opposite influences: the traditions of the magazine, stretching back into the more conservative period of Holland's general editorship, and the radical impulses of the new realistic fiction. Since the two influences were largely irreconcilable, much of Gilder's effort was spent in choosing between them—and even more of it was dedicated to justifying his position in *having* to choose between them.

As an editor, Gilder could recognize talent or genius no matter what philosophy it was derived from; or, within limits, what facets of life it detailed. If forced, on occasion, to bow to the wishes of the audience for which he edited, he understood that he was doing so, and he did not value less the genius that was sacrificed for his action. In the personal tug-of-war that was his position as editor of *The Century,* he surrendered more to the demands of his readers and the traditions of the magazine than he wished, but he was always aware that he was doing so. It was therefore necessary for him to justify his actions, as much for his own sensibilities as for the world's, in statements like the ones quoted above. Their defensiveness derives from the fact that the situation was not of his choosing. He knew as well as the writers who complained about the editorial policies of the magazine that there was an inequality in the prestige and payment for the common variety of magazine fiction as compared to literature. He could only point out in his own defense that literature, even of the most radical kind, could find some audience somewhere, and that the author need not go entirely unrewarded. For his own part, he continued to try as he wrote to Henry James on May 29, 1883, "to be a good way in advance of the multitude and to insist upon the literary view and upon a decided freedom of discussion" (GP).

IV *International Copyright*

Beyond defending his own editorial position, Gilder had only one area of reform in the literary situation of America available for direct, positive action—the movement towards international copyright legislation. To that movement he devoted much of his energy during the most fruitful years of his life.

For a century before an international copyright treaty was signed in 1891, American writers suffered from an enormous loss of income because of pirated English editions of their own works published in this country and especially by competition with books by English authors pirated by American publishers. Writers with unestablished reputations in particular were at a disadvantage with American publishers who could print works of established and popular English authors for token royalty payments or no royalties at all. From the American writers' point of view, the situation was intolerable; and the enactment of international copyright legislation represented the most obvious first step toward national literary integrity.

Gilder, sensitive to his own false position in the economics of literature, saw an international copyright treaty as the *sine qua non* for a healthy American literature long before such a position became fashionable. He was one of the founders of the American Copyright League, the lobbying organization that eventually included nearly all of the country's best writers, and that was directly responsible for the passage of the treaty bill. Even before the founding of the League, he worked actively towards influencing members of Congress to favor copyright legislation. His efforts, for more than a decade, were wholehearted and included every conceivable opportunity and medium to advance the cause. Almost any speech Gilder gave on whatever subject before 1891 includes something about copyright. No less then seven scrapbooks were filled by Gilder with clippings from every periodical that would accept his letters on the subject.[10] Not the least of his contributions to the movement was to free his associate editor, Robert Underwood Johnson, from all editorial responsibilities for three years to enable him to reside in Washington as a lobbyist for the American Copyright League.

The passage of the treaty bill must surely have been the greatest single victory of Gilder's life. When he placed the need for international copyright next to the Sermon on the Mount in a letter to Hamlin Garland quoted in Chapter Five, he was not entirely in jest. Perhaps he oversimplified the problem of the American writer's economic position in his eagerness to have the treaty accepted; but the bill, "his" bill, was unquestionably the only significant legal advancement toward American literary independence in the entire nineteenth century. It is not the lot of most human beings to participate in a crusade, especially in a *successful* one. Gilder took part in many, from housing reforms in New York City to the cession of the valley of the Yosemite to control by the federal government as a National Park, from Civil Service reform to women's rights. But international copyright was always his most important crusade, tied as it was in his mind with the condition of the American writer. He experienced the success of the movement in 1891, but he really did not live long enough to gauge the total effect of the new legislation upon American letters. Gilder tried to believe that the situation had been alleviated. His public statements after 1891 are less defensive about the position of the magazine in literature, more optimistic for the future of American writers, since the market for their work expanded once the treaty passed. Nevertheless, the great changes in American literature, at least partially made possible by the treaty bill, either did not occur until after his death or appeared so gradually that he could not have been aware of them. Even this greatest success of his life had within it, therefore, an element of disappointment.

V *The Decline of* The Century

Gilder's critical writings on the three central topics of his age are all in some measure disappointing—disappointing to the modern reader's perspective, and, ultimately, evidence of disappointment on the part of Gilder himself. His career was perhaps too long and spanned too revolutionary a period; his critical ideas, formed in the 1870's and 1880's, were not quite flexible enough to answer to the new situation of the 1890's and the first decade of a new century. Also, Gilder's critical decline is connected closely with the decline of the magazine he edited. Tied for life to *The Century,* Gilder, in his critical writings, reflects the state of the magazine; and the story of the decline of the magazine suggests as well that of its editor.

The period of blossom for *The Century* was the decade 1880–90. During those years the magazine achieved its highest peak in the quality of its publications, the liberality of its views, and—not unrelated—the extent of its circulation. The February, 1885, issue, in which sections from Howells' *The Rise of Silas Lapham,* Twain's *Huckleberry Finn,* and James' *The Bostonians* all appeared, provides a symbolic apogee of the magazine's fortunes. Indeed, that one issue represents probably the greatest twenty-five cents worth of original American literature in the history of American periodicals. Thereafter, the magazine declined; and, although it continued to exercise great power and prestige through Gilder's lifetime, the last twenty years of his life were spent attempting to halt a progressive decrease in circulation and prestige.

Gilder did not become appreciably more conservative in his approach to literature as he grew older; instead, literature became more radically frank and materialistic. Faced with a choice of betraying his ideals and of printing material that he feared would tend to be morally degenerative, or of retreating to more romantic but sub-literary fiction, Gilder retreated. Gilder felt the obligation to his audience, which grew smaller and smaller as a new generation chose to subscribe to magazines that had less prestige and typographic distinction than *The Century*, but greater liberality in their choice of fiction. The smiling realism of Howells was replaced by a more snarling variety by writers like Dreiser and Norris; the new magazines, mass-produced and inexpensive, were not only willing to print all they could get of the New Realism, but also to pay better for it than *The Century* could. Nor did Gilder succeed with these writers as he did with Garland in publishing their less sordid work, for the writers tended to stay with magazines that could provide a constant market. Only Jack London, among the New Realists, saw fit to prostitute himself to the staid old *Century* with a major work, *The Sea Wolf*.

Gilder's lack of sympathy with the newer writers was not the only reason for the decline of *The Century*. Another factor was the more prominent editorial position of Robert Underwood Johnson as Gilder retired from office routines. Just as Gilder had exerted increasing editorial influence over *Scribner's Monthly* during Holland's last years, so Johnson made his presence felt as he absorbed increasing editorial power. The difference was that Gilder had been a liberal influence on Holland, while Johnson was probably the most prudish editor on the staff of *The Century*. One of his colleagues observed that "of all the editorial force, [Johnson] was easily the most conservative follower of good form— good form in literature, good form in one's social relations. Indeed, in a private catechism of his own the first rule appeared to be not so much to glorify God and enjoy Him forever as to observe all the amenities of life." [11]

Johnson's editorial timidity is well documented. He opposed Gilder on the serialization James Lane Allen's novel, *The Reign of Law*, on the grounds that, "however delicately" the motive was treated, it would "still be impossible to talk about it to young people" (CC, Jan. 18, 1898). A more serious aberration was his opposition to Edith Wharton's work. Gilder admired her novels and wished to make her a protegée of *The Century*, but he was unable to convince Johnson that her talent as a writer was sufficient compensation for the editorial risks involved in publishing her work. One letter from Gilder to Johnson on the subject of Mrs. Wharton illustrates Gilder's enthusiasm, Johnson's prudishness, and Johnson's prominence as an editorial force on the magazine: "I'm sorry you don't feel as I do about Mrs. Wharton's position as a story writer. . . . In her Harper and other stories touching on divorce she is very strong and human; as well as being a writer—which few of our novelists are. . . . She is on the eve of a great popular success such as Mrs. Ward has made, I think, and I fear that we will not then be able to get her. I had an idea that we could develop her fame and make a good thing in every way out of both serial and book publication. But I will go slow on account of your feeling" (GP, Aug. 20, 1904).

The letter is pathetic in several ways. By 1904 the prestige of *The Century* had waned to such a point that it is doubtful that Edith Wharton would have accepted an invitation to write exclusively for the magazine anyway. Worse, the picture of Gilder supplicating his associate editor on a question of basic editorial policy suggests that *The Century* had indeed fallen on evil days. Perhaps therein lies the secret of the decline of the magazine; simply that the otherwise brilliant Roswell Smith failed to perpetuate one of the conditions of the success of *Scribner's Monthly* in the founding of *The Century*—that the associate editor ought to be of a younger generation than the editor. At any rate, the decline of the magazine did not cease during Gilder's lifetime, nor during Johnson's succession, nor at all until its final foundering in the 1920's. In effect, the greatness of the magazine did not outlast the greatness of its first editor.

VI *Liberal Editor, Genteel Age*

Alfred Kazin's opinion of Gilder is typical of many, perhaps most, modern critics and literary historians who treat Gilder as a symbol of the Genteel Tradition, whether nor not they use the specific word:[12]

> The Genteel Tradition, which a later generation was to flog long after it had become a dead horse, was a very real thing . . . under the custodianship of such editors as Richard Watson Gilder. Gilder, who liked to call himself a "squire of poesy," wrote sixteen volumes of verse and served as an editor at *Scribner's* [*Monthly*] and the *Century* for thirty-nine years, was a very amiable man whom some malicious fortune set up as a perfect symbol of all that the new writers were to detest.

Gilder was much more than that. As a force in the development of American literature, he is important both for his promotion of

American writing generally, for his perceptive editing and encouragement of thousands of American writers over a period of forty years, and for the editorial genius with which he supported such writers as Whitman, Cable, Howells and Twain. And his influence was almost entirely on American writers. Indeed, perhaps his greatest service was to provide in *The Century* a market devoted almost exclusively to American productions.

At the same time he contributed to the literary self-respect of American writers by defending personally and editorially his policy and American literature. He performed this service at the expense of popularity for the magazine and at the cost of subordinating his own personal esthetic on many occasions. He stated his position and the rationale behind it in a letter to Edmund Gosse refusing the use of *The Century*'s pages for a regular series of English contributions: " 'The Century' is not purely literary, purely artistic, nor purely altruistic and reformatory. . . . You say we should 'get the best'. . . . Suppose we should carry out to the utmost this idea of getting the best. It is my suspicion that the best writer of fiction today is Tolstoi. . . . Why should we not try to get him to write novels for the Century? Which should we do, publish his novels or Cable's? Instead of this we get Kennan to . . . see him and write an article about him which will interest all intelligent readers . . . of America" (GP, Mar. 7, 1887).

Gilder's was a self-conscious Americanism and literary esthetic. He was aware of the necessity for "imperfection" in his magazine. Given the choice between even first-rate English writing and second-rate American writing, his decision was, more often than not, for the American product. Given the choice between literature and popular magazine material, it was for literature. A rational man, he realized that all such choices are necessarily of imperfections; and, if the magazine must be imperfect, it could at least serve the greater purpose of being literate and American. What his attitude meant to American literature can hardly be estimated. We need not agree with his critical viewpoint—indeed, we may point out dozens of cases where his critical judgment was at fault; but we must conclude that he performed a valuable, a necessary service.

Richard Watson Gilder suffered from many of the limitations of his age. He could be a prude, his critical ideas were often conservative, he sometimes did serve as a bastion for the "genteel tradition." He was not, however, a symbol; he was an intelligent critic and editor and, what is perhaps more important, a man aware of his own limitations and the limitations of his age. He may continue to be remembered as the man who found Crane's *Maggie* "too honest," and who told Cable to take " 'Posson' Jone" elsewhere —editorial miscalculations that could probably be multiplied a hundred times in his own case—and just as often for every other editor who ever took a blue pencil to a manuscript or wrote a letter of rejection. But Gilder should also be remembered for the real services he performed for American literature and for the many instances when his judgment was correct, when his vision exceeded that of his own age, and when his courage was extended beyond his own limits. He was certainly a great editor. American literature is the richer for him.

Notes and References

Chapter One

1. Holland to Gilder, July 27 and August 15, 1870, in the papers of R. W. Gilder, Miss Rosamond Gilder, New York City. Hereafter cited in the text as "GP."

2. Robert Underwood Johnson, *Remembered Yesterdays* (Boston, 1923), p. 87; Holland to Charles Scribner, October 15, 1869, Scribner Company archives.

3. Roger Burlingame, *Of Making Many Books* (New York, 1946), p. 199; Frank L. Mott, *A History of American Magazines* (Cambridge, Mass., 1938), III, 20.

4. Robert Berkleman, "Mrs. Grundy and Richard Watson Gilder," *American Quarterly*, IV (1952), 67; R. W. Gilder, "The Newspaper, the Magazine, and the Public," *Outlook*, LXI (February 4, 1899), 319.

5. Johnson, p. 97.

6. Rosamond Gilder, ed., *Letters of Richard Watson Gilder* (Boston and New York, 1916), pp. 392–3, 397. Hereafter cited in the text as "LRWG."

7. *Scribner's Monthly*, I (November, 1870), 106.

8. L. Frank Tooker, *The Joys and Tribulations of an Editor* (New York, 1924), p. 54.

9. Quoted in Joyce Kilmer, *Literature in the Making* (New York, 1917), p. 8.

10. Gilder to Charles G. Leland, January 5, 1880, letterpress copy in the Gilder Letterbooks, New York Public Library. Hereafter cited in the text as "GL."

11. *The Century*, XXIII (November, 1881), 143; XXXV (Nov., 1887), 160. Hereafter, all citations from *Scribner's Monthly* and *The Century* are given by volume and page number in the text.

12. Tooker, pp. 67, 74.

13. *LRWG*, p. 387; See also, for example, Gilder to Edna Kenton, February 24, 1906, Kenton Papers, Columbia University Library.

14. Verses inscribed to R. R. Bowker in a copy of Gilder's *The New Day* (New York, 1876), dated October 12, 1875, in the collection of the Stockbridge (Mass.) Library Association. The verses are a parody of Gilder's "When I am Dead and Buried," first printed in *Scribner's Monthly*, V (April, 1873), 766–67, reprinted in *Poems of Richard*

Watson Gilder (Boston and New York, 1908), p. 80. Cited hereafter in the text as "Poems."

15. R. W. Gilder, "An 'Open Letter' about Editing," *Independent*, XLVIII (Dec. 10, 1896), 1870.

16. John Bigelow to Gilder, March 28, 1892, Century Collection, New York Public Library. Cited hereafter in the text as "CC."

17. Tooker, p. 179.

Chapter Two

1. April 4, 1892, Stedman Papers, Columbia University Library.

2. Gilder to Stedman, Aug. 20 and Sept. 15, 1873, Stedman Papers.

3. Robinson to Gilder, December 22, 1908, E. A. Robinson Collection, New York Public Library.

4. James L. Onderdonk, *History of American Verse (1610–1897)* (Chicago, 1901), pp. 368–9.

5. Lewisohn, pp. 91–93. For a possible reason for Lewisohn's singling out Gilder as his example of the worst of the poets of his day, see his letters to Gilder in the Century Collection.

6. Robinson to Gilder, March 23 and April 11, 1905, Robinson Collection.

7. Horace Traubel, ed., *With Walt Whitman in Camden*, 4 v. (Boston and New York, 1906–1914), I, 184. Cited hereafter in the text as "WWW"

8. Johnson, pp. 337–38.

9. *Ibid.* See also Laura Stedman and George M. Gould, eds., *Life and Letters of Edmund Clarence Stedman*, 2 v. (New York, 1910), II, 106, 109–10.

10. WWW, II, 118–9. Gilder, one of the few American members of the Societé des Félibriges, a group of Provençal poets headed by Mistral, had arranged the translation with Wyse.

11. See Gilder to Whitman, GL, June 7, 1883; WWW, II, 166. The "other writer" was actually Charles DeKay, Gilder's brother-in-law, a poet who received almost no attention during his lifetime and whose verse Gilder admired inordinately. In the Gilder Papers is a pocket-sized copy of *Leaves of Grass*, tattered beyond belief. Rosamond Gilder has said, and the condition of the book bears her out, that her father carried it with him everywhere and would read passages from it to friends or strangers at every opportunity.

12. Quoted in Horace L. Traubel, ed., *Camden's Compliment to Walt Whitman* (Philadelphia, 1889), pp. 37–38. Further citations given in the text. When Gilder said he admired Whitman's "magnificent form," Whitman looked up at him in surprise, saying, "well, well, do *you* say that?" LRWG, p. 186.

13. Probably "Self-reverence, self-knowledge, self-control,—/These three alone lead life to sovereign power," *Œnone*. But see also *In Memoriam* LV and CXXX.

14. See *WWW*, II, 212–13; Portia Baker, "Walt Whitman's Relations with Some New York Magazines," *American Literature*, VII (1935), 274–301, *passim*. The tone of Miss Baker's article suggests that Holland's influence was still paramount on *The Century*, even, sometimes, that he lived beyond 1881. She also exhibits some confusion between *Scribner's Monthly* (*The Century*) and *Scribner's Magazine*.

Chapter Three

1. "The Development of Southern Literature," a speech written by Gilder about 1880 and delivered on several occasions during the next decade. Parts of it were published in *The Christian Advocate* for July 3, 1890. My quotations are from the original manuscript in the Gilder Papers.

2. Samuel C. Chew, *Fruit Among Leaves* (New York, 1950), pp. 83–84; Jay B. Hubbell, *The South in American Literature* (Durham, N. C., 1954), p. 728.

3. Page to Gilder, March 31, 1885, Thomas Nelson Page Collection, Alderman Library, University of Virginia. Hereafter cited in the text as "PC."

4. Gilder to Harris, Mar. 10, 1881, Harris Papers, Emory University Library. Hereafter cited in the text as "HP."

5. Quoted in Julia Collier Harris, *The Life and Letters of Joel Chandler Harris* (Boston and New York, 1918), p. 186. Hereafter cited in the text as "*LJCH*".

6. Quoted in Johnson, p. 381.

7. *Ibid.*, p. 383.

8. Harris to Gilder, March 12 [1887], miscellaneous manuscript letter in the collection of the Library of the University of Rochester. The letter is undated, but from internal evidence clearly relates to this story.

9. Hubbell, p. 793.

10. His only published work before Gilder discovered him were sketches written for New Orleans newspapers. See Arlin Turner, *George Washington Cable, A Biography* (Durham, N. C., 1956), p. 50. In 1871 Cable sent a bundle of clippings of his writings for the New Orleans *Picayune* to Scribner, Armstrong, and Company, just downstairs from the offices of *Scribner's Monthly*, with an offer to help pay for their publication. Charles Scribner rejected them. See Burlingame, p. 49.

11. Lucy Cable Biklé, *George Washington Cable, His Life and Letters* (New York and London, 1928), p. 49.

12. Quoted in Kjell Ekstrom, *George Washington Cable, A Study of His Early Life and Work* (Upsala, Cambridge, Mass., 1950), p. 96.

13. Turner, p. 68. Turner's summary of Gilder's influence on Cable (pp. 67–69) during these earliest years is reasoned and sound, with generally just criticisms and a basic understanding of the problems Gilder faced.

14. GL, Feb. 1, 1882. *LRWG* has a truncated version of this letter, omitting the name of the recipient and the title of the work criticized, pp. 389–91.

15. Grace King, *Memories of a Southern Woman of Letters* (New York, 1932), p. 59.

16. Gilder to Cable, March 13, 1889, Cable Papers, Tulane University Library.

17. Hubbell, p. 818; Turner, pp. 291–2.

Chapter Four

1. Anonymous, "American Literature in England," *Blackwood's Magazine*, CXXXIII (Jan., 1883), 138.

2. Gosse to Gilder, March 18, 1887, Gosse Collection, Houghton Library, Harvard University.

3. Tooker, p. 227.

4. *The Rise of Silas Lapham* was running concurrently with *The Bostonians* in *The Century*.

5. Letter of August 25, 1915, quoted in Percy Lubbock, ed., *The Letters of Henry James*, vol. II (New York, 1920), II, 498.

Chapter Five

1. See Geoffrey Bret Harte, ed., *The Letters of Bret Harte* (Boston and New York, 1936), pp. 51–2, 110–11.

2. Tooker, p. 244; Edward Eggleston, *Duffels* (New York, 1893), p. vi.

3. See Bernard I. Duffey, "Hamlin Garland's 'Decline' from Realism," *American Literature*, XXV (1953), 69–74; James D. Koerner, "Comment on 'Hamlin Garland's "Decline" from Realism,'" *Ibid.*, XXVI (1954), 427–32; and Duffey's "Mr. Koerner's Reply considered," *Ibid.*, XXVI (1954), 432–35. Both writers assume that Gilder's influence upon Garland was harmful; they differ on the question of Garland's *willingness* to be emasculated. Donald Pizer, *Hamlin Garland's Early*

Work and Career (Berkeley and Los Angeles, 1960), esp. pp. 64–9, has a deeper insight into Gilder's relations with Garland.

4. Garland to Gilder, June [1889], Garland Collection, New York Public Library. Cited hereafter in the text as "GC."

5. Pizer, pp. 64, 182; Hamlin Garland, *A Son of the Middle Border* (New York, 1938), p. 412.

6. Quoted in Eldon C. Hill, "A Biographical Study of Hamlin Garland from 1860 to 1895" (unpublished Ph.D. dissertation, Ohio State University, 1940), pp. 116–17.

7. GC, n.d., but written April 2 or 3, 1890.

8. Hamlin Garland, *Roadside Meetings* (New York, 1930), p. 182.

9. Quoted entirely in Hill, 119–20, partially in Garland, *Roadside Meetings*, pp. 182–3.

10. Quoted in Hill, pp. 120–22. The book referred to is James G. Blaine's *Twenty Years of Congress: From Lincoln to Garfield.* Blaine's name was actually used in the story as it appeared in the magazine, doubtless because the story did not appear in *The Century* until seven years after this correspondence (LIII, 402–23). Of the editorial suggestions in this letter, only the last deletion (number 7) was actually made in the story, though all the corrections were kept.

11. Garland, *Roadside Meetings*, p. 335.

Chapter Six

1. Gilder to Howells, January 19, 1874, Howells Papers, Houghton Library, Harvard University. Hereafter cited as "HP" in the text.

2. This was George P. Fisher's "The Revised New Testament," *Scribner's Monthly*, XXII (June, 1881), 293–301.

3. HP, Oct. 19 and Sept. 3, 1881. Gilder suggested February, 1882, as a beginning date, but later preferred an earlier date when Howells failed to write a play he had earlier promised Gilder.

4. Edwin H. Cady, *The Road to Realism; The Early Years, 1837–1885, of William Dean Howells* (Syracuse, N.Y., 1956), p. 218, mentions this point but gives no suggestion as to how the "able team of Roswell Smith . . . and Richard Watson Gilder" managed "to snatch the leading position among American magazines for the *Century*."

5. See Robert W. Walts, "William Dean Howells and the House of Harper" (unpublished Ph.D. dissertation, Rutgers University, 1953), pp. 23–6.

6. XXIV, 940. Howells agreed with Gilder's interpretation of the novel. He wrote that he was glad Gilder had "insisted upon its [*A Modern Instance's*] treatment of the whole marriage relation rather than its bearing on the divorce question," adding that the divorce ele-

ment "became more and more incidental" as he progressed with the novel. Howells to Gilder, Oct. 24, 1882, Daniel Coit Gilman Papers, The Johns Hopkins University Library.

7. GL, Dec. 22, 1883. The "lost novel" was *Indian Summer*, serialized in *Harper's Monthly*, July, 1885, to February, 1886.

8. For a summary of the plot as Howells envisaged it in 1883, see Rudolf and Clara Kirk, *William Dean Howells, Representative Selections* (American Writers Series, New York, 1950), pp. cix–cx.

9. John Bigelow, "Some Recollections of Charles O'Connor," *The Century*, XXIX (1885), 725–36. The article is generally sympathetic with Irish Nationalist activities, as was *The Century's* general editorial policy.

10. HP, February 18, 1885, partially quoted in Van Wyck Brooks, *Howells: His Life and World* (New York, 1959), pp. 88–9. A letter of Roswell Smith to Howells on the same date seconded Gilder's objections. Corrections were received from Howells two days later.

11. Gilman Papers, July 6, 1882, The Johns Hopkins University Library.

Chapter Seven

1. Albert B. Paine, ed., *Mark Twain's Autobiography* (New York and London, 1924), I, 31–9, *passim*; LRWG, p. 124; Johnson pp. 217–218.

2. Albert B. Paine, *Mark Twain, A Biography* (New York and London, 1912), III, 1252, 1332. Gilder's remarks at the seventieth-birthday dinner were printed in a supplement to *Harper's Weekly*, (Dec. 23, 1905), pp. 1887–8.

3. See Gilder to Stanford White, GL, April 15, 1906, for his part in the Gorky affair. Miss Gilder's memories of Twain were personally communicated to me.

4. Doubtless because *Huckleberry Finn* is such a great work and because the truncated excerpts in *The Century* provide an unusually good opportunity to see what a "genteel" editor could do to Twain's unruly genius, two critics, Bernard DeVoto in *Mark Twain's America* (Boston, 1932), pp. 212–16, and Arthur L. Scott in "*The Century Magazine* Edits *Huckleberry Finn*, 1884–85," *American Literature*, XXVII (Nov., 1955), 356–62, compared *The Century's* excerpts with the book text to see what had been changed. DeVoto's purpose was to show that only verbal, not philosophical changes had been made, and that Twain emerged nearly unscathed from the ordeal. Scott, who, though he duplicates many of DeVoto's comments, never cites the earlier work, was trying to prove that Gilder "crammed Mark Twain's sprawling narrative into something more or less resembling the chaste,

urbane, conventional mold of its two bedfellows—*The Bostonians* and *The Rise of Silas Lapham*" (362).

Both men made three errors which vitiate their conclusions: first, they inclined to treat the three excerpts as a single unit, not as individual contributions, as Gilder intended them to be read; second, they forgot or ignored the purely physical problems of magazine publication, especially the editor's concern over the length of each article in terms of the space available; third, they show no awareness of Gilder's purpose in the publication of the three excerpts. In addition, neither man consulted the Mark Twain Papers for the supplemental information available there. (In DeVoto's favor, it ought to be noted that, when he wrote, he was denied the use of Twain's papers; the same cannot be said about Scott.) While most of their facts are correct, their conclusions are almost invariably wrong. To save citations, I am not noting the specific incorrect judgments of either critic; but I urge the reader to consult these two works to judge for himself.

5. The other instance was also a work by Mark Twain, *A Connecticut Yankee in King Arthur's Court.* Gilder's treatment of that work is discussed below.

6. I would feel more self-conscious about pointing out such obvious facts were it not for the propensity of irresponsible critics to ignore them. Jerry Allen, for example, in *The Adventures of Mark Twain* (Boston, 1954), p. 268, gives the dignity of print to the absurd notion that Twain's "red temper flared at the demands of Gilder's prudery and when he published *Huckleberry Finn* he spurned the *Century's* careful editing and issued the book as he wrote it."

7. DeVoto, p. 214, incorrectly includes this remark among Gilder's deletions.

8. Gilder to Twain, October 10, 1884, Mark Twain Papers, University of California Library, Berkeley.

9. The most complete discussion of the phallic character of the incident is in B. J. Whiting, "Guyuscutus, Royal Nonesuch, and Other Hoaxes," *Southern Folklore Quarterly*, VIII (Dec., 1944), 251–75.

10. Samuel C. Webster, *Mark Twain, Business Man* (Boston, 1946), p. 292.

11. Arthur L. Vogelback, "The Publication and Reception of *Huckleberry Finn* in America," *American Literature*, XI (Nov., 1939), 267.

12. XXX, 172–3. The style and content of this statement are so similar to other comments made by Gilder on the same subject that I am convinced that Gilder either wrote the passage himself or at least outlined the comment for Perry.

13. Albert Barrère and Charles G. Leland, *A Dictionary of Slang, Jargon, and Cant* (London, 1890), II, 201–2.

Chapter Eight

1. R. W. Gilder, "Certain Tendencies in Current Literature," *New Princeton Review*, IV (July, 1887), 6. References to this essay are cited hereafter as *NPR* in the text.

2. Gilder sent a copy of this article to Howells with a letter which expresses both his debt to Howells' idea and his independent position on the subject of realism in literature. He wrote: "If there is anything you don't like in my screed (written to be *spoken*, remember) put it down to heredity—a Methodist preacher's son! But I learn this from you—literary frankness;—it is to be our salvation! I quarrel a good deal with some of your opinions, so exquisitely, sometimes magnificently expressed in the [Editor's] Study—but you are, I know, whipping a lazy horse uphill! I quarrel, I say & yet I hold out my hand to you as a voice crying in the wilderness. With all its qualifications & protests & leanings toward something else, I hope you will find in my essay more sympathy than your critics give for the new movement." HP, July 14, 1887.

3. Thomas Beer, *Stephen Crane, A Study in American Letters* (New York, 1924), pp. 83–6. Beer gives no source for the incident, but does give very specific dates (March 23, 1892, for the confrontation in Gilder's office, 1904, for an interview in which Gilder explained his action). In the light of Gilder's character and the content of *Maggie*, the incident as described by Beer has the ring of truth.

4. Gilder, "An 'Open Letter,'" *Independent, loc. cit.*, 1670.

5. "The Development of Southern Literature," GP.

6. John Hay Papers, Brown University Library, June 30, 1882.

7. The quotation is from *An Apology against . . . Smectymnuus* (Milford C. Jochanus, ed., Urbana, Ill., 1960), p. 32.

8. GL, June 24, 1907. Viereck printed the letter in "Some Recollections of Richard Watson Gilder," *The Forum*, XLIII (Jan., 1910), 77, with paragraphs three and six deleted and, strangely, the Milton quotation corrupted. *Nineveh* was published in New York in 1907. Viereck was associated with Gilder both as a poet and for a time as a member of *The Century* staff.

9. In a speech on "Journalism and American Literature," quoted in *The Critic*, n.s., XV (Feb. 7, 1891), 71. All the quotations in this and the next paragraph are from this source.

10. The scrapbooks are part of the Gilder Letterbook collection in the New York Public Library. The Gilder Letterbooks have one complete series of five volumes, 1885–1891, a total of some five thousand letters, relating entirely to copyright legislation and the lobbying activities of Gilder and others of *The Century* staff.

11. Tooker, p. 61.

12. Alfred Kazin, *On Native Grounds* (New York, 1942), p. 56. While the bulk of critical opinion treats Gilder unsympathetically, there are of course exceptions. Edward Wagenknecht, "Richard Watson Gilder: Poet and Editor of the Transition," *Boston University Studies in English*, I (1955), 84–95, and Robert Berkleman, "Mrs. Grundy and Richard Watson Gilder," *American Quarterly*, IV (1952), 66–72, treat Gilder perceptively. Both articles provided stimulus for this study.

Selected Bibliography

PRIMARY SOURCES

1. *Manuscript Sources*:

Gilder Papers. Letters received and copies of letters by Richard Watson Gilder, in the possession of Miss Rosamond Gilder, New York City.

Gilder Letterbooks. Letterpress copies of letters sent by Gilder from the Century Company offices, twenty-one volumes in two series, in the New York Public Library.

Century Papers. The archives of the Century Company. Two hundred and seven boxes of letters received from contributors, subscribers, and agents of the company. The files are unfortunately incomplete; many of the letters received were separated from the archives and sold at an auction held by the Anderson Galleries, New York, December 3 and 4, 1928. New York Public Library.

Holland Papers. Papers of Josiah G. Holland, incomplete, but useful for the period 1870–1880. New York Public Library.

Garland Collection. Letters of Hamlin Garland to the editors of *The Century Magazine*. New York Public Library.

R. R. Bowker Papers. New York Public Library.

Edwin Arlington Robinson Papers. New York Public Library.

Edmund Clarence Stedman Papers. Columbia University Library.

William Dean Howells Papers. Houghton Library, Harvard University.

George Washington Cable Papers. Tulane University Library.

Mark Twain Papers. University of California Library, Berkeley.

In addition, the *Checklist of Holdings of American Literary Manuscripts in . . . Libraries of the United States,* prepared by the Committee on Manuscript Holdings of the Modern Language Association lists forty-six libraries with holdings of manuscripts relating to Gilder.

2. *Printed Sources*:

The basic printed sources for this study are *Scribner's Monthly Magazine,* vols. I–XXII, November, 1870 to October, 1881, and *The Century Illustrated Monthly Magazine,* Vols. XXIII–LXXIX, November,

1881, to February, 1910. Much of Gilder's writing appears within the magazine; much more may be found in other periodicals and books. Among the latter, the following are particularly significant.

"Certain Tendencies in Current Literature," *New Princeton Review*, IV (July, 1887), 1–20.

"Journalism and American Literature," *The Critic*, n.s., XV (Feb. 7, 1891), 71.

Letters of Richard Watson Gilder. Rosamond Gilder, ed. Boston and New York: Houghton Mifflin, 1916.

"Mark Twain: A Glance at His Spoken and Written Art," *Outlook*, LXXVIII (December 3, 1904), 842–44.

"The Newspaper, the Magazine, and the Public," *Outlook*, LXI (Feb. 4, 1899), 317–21.

"An 'Open Letter' about Editing," *Independent*, XLVIII (Dec. 10, 1896), 1669–70.

Poems of Richard Watson Gilder. Boston and New York: Houghton Mifflin, 1908.

SECONDARY SOURCES

Most critical appraisals of Gilder are derivative. The following list, exceedingly selective, includes only significant and original statements.

BERKLEMAN, ROBERT. "Mrs. Grundy and Richard Watson Gilder." *American Quarterly*, IV (1952), 66–72. Sympathetic but undocumented.

CHEW, SAMUEL C. *Fruit Among the Leaves: An Anniversary Anthology*. New York: Appleton Century-Crofts. 1950. A sympathetic history of Century Company with a balanced appraisal of Gilder.

DE VOTO, BERNARD. *Mark Twain's America*. Boston: Houghton Mifflin. 1932. See above, Chapter VII.

DOWNEY, DAVID G. *Modern Poets and Christian Teaching: Richard Watson Gilder, Edwin Markham, Edward Rowland Sill*. New York: Eaton and Mains, [c. 1906]. A typical misreading of Gilder's poetry by a contemporary.

FORD, JAMES L. *Forty-Odd Years in the Literary Shop*. New York: Dutton. 1921. Probably the original attack on Gilder as the archetypal "genteel" editor; used, but uncited, by many later critics.

KAZIN, ALFRED. *On Native Grounds*. New York: Harcourt, Brace. 1942. See above, Chapter VIII.

KINDILIEN, CARLIN T. *American Poetry in the Eighteen-Nineties*. Providence, R. I.: Brown University Press. 1956. Gilder as the idealist poet and editor of idealist poetry exclusively.

LEWISOHN, LUDWIG. *Expression in America*. New York and London: Harper. 1932. Gilder the typical poet of "the age of tin."

ONDERDONK, JAMES L. *History of American Verse (1610–1897)*. Chicago: McClurg. 1901. Uncritical and flattering about Gilder's poetry.

SCOTT, ARTHUR L. "The *Century Magazine* Edits *Huckleberry Finn,* 1884–1885," *American Literature,* XXVII (November, 1955), 356–62. See above, Chapter VII.

SMITH, HERBERT F. "Joel Chandler Harris's Contributions to *Scribner's Monthly* and *The Century Magazine,* 1880–1887," *Georgia Historical Quarterly,* XLVII (June, 1963), 169–79.

SMITH, HERBERT F. and PEINOVICH, MICHAEL. "*The Bostonians:* Creation and Revision," *Bulletin of the New York Public Library,* LXXIII (May, 1969), 298–308.

WAGENKNECHT, EDWARD C. "Richard Watson Gilder: Poet and Editor of the Transition," *Boston University Studies in English,* I (1955), 84–95. Typical of Professor Wagenknecht's "psychographs," an incisive study, but concerned more with the man than his work.

Index

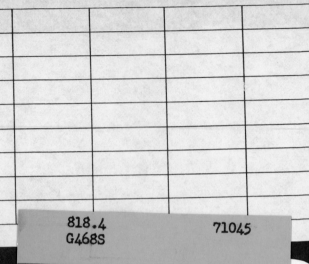